FORGERS AND CRITICS

FORGERS
AND
CRITICS

*****

*Creativity and Duplicity in
Western Scholarship*

ANTHONY GRAFTON

PRINCETON UNIVERSITY PRESS
PRINCETON, NEW JERSEY

Copyright © 1990 by Princeton University Press
Published by Princeton University Press, 41 William Street,
Princeton, New Jersey 08540
In the United Kingdom: Princeton University Press, Oxford

Library of Congress Cataloging-in-Publication Data

Grafton, Anthony.
Forgers and critics : creativity and duplicity in
western scholarship / Anthony Grafton.
p. cm.
Includes bibliographical references (p.).
ISBN 0-691-05544-0 (alk. paper)
1. Literary forgeries and mystifications—History. 2. Creation (Literary,
artistic, etc.)—History. 3. Learning and scholarship—History. 4. Criticism—
History. I. Title.
PN171.F6G74 1990
098'.3—dc20   89-28347

Publication of this book has been aided by the
Whitney Darrow Fund of Princeton University Press

This book has been composed in Linotron Sabon

Princeton University Press books are printed on acid-free paper,
and meet the guidelines for permanence and durability of the
Committee on Production Guidelines for Book Longevity
of the Council on Library Resources

Printed in the United States of America by
Princeton University Press,
Princeton, New Jersey

1 3 5 7 9 10 8 6 4 2

CONTENTS

ILLUSTRATIONS

ACKNOWLEDGMENTS

THIS ESSAY began as a Walter Edge Public Lecture at Princeton University. I should like to thank the university's Committee on Public Lectures for inviting me to speak; Edward Tenner of Princeton University Press, who suggested that the lecture might grow into a book; and Joanna Hitchcock, who guided it to completion with sympathetic firmness. Helpfully contentious audiences at Princeton University, the Warburg Institute, the Newberry Library, Columbia University, Harvard University, and the University of California at Santa Barbara challenged me on many points of fact and interpretation. I feel a special debt to Peter Brown and the other members of his Group for the Study of Late Antiquity at Princeton, who allowed me to present two sections of the book as papers; their vast learning and warm encouragement did much to make my expeditions into classical and late antique territory rewarding. Nicholas Barker, Carlotta Dionisotti, James Hankins, Glenn Most, Mac Pigman, David Quint, Nancy Siraisi, Noel Swerdlow, and Robert Westman criticized all or part of the manuscript, greatly to my benefit. Jill Kraye—for many years my companion in the study of literary crime—contributed enormously to the substance and considerably chastened the style of the whole work.

Eric Cochrane introduced me to the eternally fascinating subject of historical criticism in the summer of 1968, when I wrote a term paper on Herodotus and Thucydides under his supervision in the days that intervened between nights of an education of a different kind in the streets outside the Chicago Hilton. Eric disapproved of little books, forgers, and paradoxes, but loved all forms of dissent and debate, political and scholarly. Hence, it seems in keeping with his spirit to dedicate the book to his memory; it would certainly have stimulated one of those freewheeling arguments in which he took such pleasure, and from which all of us who studied with him derived such profit. I deeply wish that he were alive to argue with me and the shades of the forgers and critics whom I have tried to call back to life.

FORGERS AND CRITICS

INTRODUCTION

SOMETIME in the fourth century B.C., Heraclides of Pontus quarreled with another philosopher, Dionysius "the Renegade." Heraclides was a dignified, respectable, and corpulent gentleman; a student of Plato and an expert on natural philosophy, he was known by the nickname *ho pompikos*, "the stately one" (a pun on his real title, *ho pontikos*, "the one from Pontus"). Dionysius was more disreputable. Beginning as a Stoic who denied the existence of pain and pleasure, he developed an acute eye inflammation which convinced him that his principles were in error. He left his old school (hence his nickname) and spent the rest of his life—apparently a long and happy one—as a Cyrenaic, haunting bars and brothels.

Dionysius forged a tragedy, the *Parthenopaeus*, and ascribed it to Sophocles. Heraclides, who had done some forgery of his own and should have known better, duly quoted it as genuine. And Dionysius in turn proclaimed his own authorship of the work. When Heraclides insisted that it must be genuine, Dionysius pointed out that the supposed tragedy was an acrostic: the first letters of the lines spelled out the true message (in this case, the name of Dionysius' boyfriend, Pankalos). Heraclides replied that the appearance of the name could be accidental. Instructed to read on, he found that the acrostic continued with a coherent couplet:

An old monkey isn't caught by a trap.
Oh yes, he's caught at last, but it takes time.

Further initial letters spelled out a final, crushing verdict: "Heraclides is ignorant of letters." When Heraclides had read this, we are told, he blushed.[1]

In 1950, Paul Coleman-Norton of Princeton University published a new Greek fragment drawn from a set of homilies on the Gospel according to Matthew. An Oxford-trained expert on the fathers of the church, he had done original work in the 1920s on questions of authenticity and textual transmission. He said he had found his new text tucked into an Arabic manuscript in a mosque in Morocco, which he had visited during World War II in the course of Operation Torch; though the exigencies of wartime service and later friction between American soldiers and the native inhabitants of the town had prevented him from obtaining a photograph of his manuscript, he had transcribed the relevant section. This he printed in the *Catholic Biblical Quarterly* with an apparatus and extensive linguistic commentary. The text continues the passage in Matthew 24 where Jesus tells his disciples that those who are assigned the portion of the hypocrites will be condemned to "weeping and gnashing of teeth." In the new section a disciple raises an objection: what, he asks, will happen to the toothless? "O ye of little faith," Jesus replies, "teeth will be provided."[2]

Coleman-Norton never publicly claimed authorship of his text, though he suggested its comic character at numerous points in his spoof commentary, as when he offered a parallel from Lewis Copeland's *The World's Best Jokes* (1941) and remarked that the disciple who asked the question was dumb "in the Pennsylvania German sense." But he did know that students who had heard him make the same joke in his courses would recognize that he—like Dionysius the Renegade—had invented, not discovered, his apparently ancient text.[3] The modern professional scholar and the ancient barroom philosopher shared aspirations with regard to their earliest readers (whom they hoped to fool) and to the past (which they tried to recreate by a combination of technical skill and vivid imagination).

These curious cases enclose like wobbly bookends a far longer than five-foot shelf of forgeries, one which stretches, as the dates of the forgeries suggest, from the beginnings of Western civilization to the present. For 2,500 years and more, forgery has amused its uninvolved observers, enraged its humiliated victims, flourished as a literary genre and, most oddly of all, stimulated vital innovations in the technical methods of scholars. Forgery has been widespread in time and place and varied in its goals and methods, and it can easily be confused with superficially similar activities. At one extremity, as in the two cases we began with, it borders on mystification, the production of literary works meant to deceive for a short time only, as practical jokes. At the other, it borders on normal fiction. Forgery does not include all works wrongly attributed to authors, since in antiquity and the Middle Ages, and even to some extent in modern times, works have been misattributed for many reasons, some quite innocent. It does not even include all works that authors have deliberately ascribed to persons other than themselves. In some periods and traditions writers have ascribed religious texts to divine or semidivine figures not because they were preoccupied with matters of authorship but because they wished to stress the continuity of their writings with an original tradition or an orthodox doctrine. A number of Jewish writers did this in the last centuries B.C. when they wrote apocalyptic and other works under the names of the biblical patriarchs, perhaps to fill the gap left by the cessation of prophecy. Such practices need not imply an intention to deceive, though they sometimes do; their products should be called pseudepigrapha rather than forgeries until the *mens rea* of the author is established.[4] In more modern times, of course, pen names have concealed a variety of sins and authors—and sometimes, as in the case of the mass of pamphlets dubiously ascribed to Defoe by nineteenth- and twentieth-century scholars, they have confused a multitude of librarians and readers.[5]

Subtracting all the pseudepigrapha not produced by forgery, however, we still confront a variegated mass of texts. Forgers have produced thousands of documents that deceived the readers for whom they were intended. Forgeries have often played a central role in religious, political, and literary history. And forgery has stimulated, both in the forgers who tried to create convincing documents and in the critics who tried to unmask them, the development of a richer sense of what the past was really like. Forger and critic have been entangled through time like Laocoon and his serpents; the changing nature of their continuous struggle forms a central theme in the development of historical and philological scholarship.

In this essay I will try to capture and display some of the splendid, evanescent triumphs of learning and style that Western forgers and critics have produced. Limits naturally have to be set on the field to be covered. I will consider, in the first place, only serious forgeries that include textual matter. Ordinary forgeries done without skill—like the Hitler diaries crudely assembled by Konrad Kujau, or the 27,345 letters by Caesar, Cleopatra, Vercingetorix, Alcuin, Alexander the Great, and Attila, among others, all written in imitation old French by Vrain-Lucas for a single client, the compliant mathematician Michel Chasles—will make no appearance here.[6] Forged works of art that include no written matter will receive no attention, forged legal documents not much. And the rich crops of literary deceit sown, irrigated, and brought to ripeness by rabbis, imams, and Chinese literati will necessarily evade the sickle of a harvester whose training is all Western. These limitations, on the other hand, will make it possible to treat a big subject in a small compass. My chief aim is to suggest by offering a combination of overview and case studies the extent, the coherence, and the historical interest of two complex, central, tightly intertwined strands in the Western tradition.

** 1 **

FORGERY AND CRITICISM:
AN OVERVIEW

FORGERY of a kind is as old as textual authority. An Egyptian wisdom text transcribed in the Middle Kingdom ends with the claim that "it has come successfully (to its end, from) its beginning to its end, like that which was found in writing"—that is, that the writer had copied accurately the ancient exemplars before him. Egyptian medical documents claim to have been found "under the feet of Anubis" or "in the night, fallen into the court of the temple in *Koptos*, as a mystery of this goddess [Isis]."[1] And the high priest Hilkiah induced good King Josiah to repent, remove the vessels of Baal from the temple, and put down the idolatrous priests in the high places not by his personal authority but by that of the book of the law which, he told Shaphan the scribe, he had "found in the house of the Lord" where all but he had missed it (2 Kings 22:8; cf. 23:1).[2] Claims of faithfulness in copying suggest, and tales of texts discovered in miraculous circumstances directly reveal, the presence of the forger.

In Greece in the sixth and fifth centuries B.C., where the Homeric epics offered the fullest account anyone had of earlier history, the Athenian statesmen Solon and Pisistratus were suspected of interpolating lines into Homer to magnify the importance of Athens. By the sixth century, as authors ceased to claim divine authority for their words, they invented human authoritative sources for facts and texts. The mythographer and historian Acusilaus of Argos supported his rich account of gods and demigods and men by asserting that he drew it from bronze tablets discovered by his father in their garden. He thereby created one of the great topoi of Western forgery, the motif of the object found in an inaccessible place, then copied, and now lost, as the authority for what would have lacked credibility as the work of an individual.[3] The historian Ctesias supported his gossipy account of Persian history—one which systematically contradicted the imperfect but far more accurate account of Herodotus—by claiming that it came from documents preserved in the archives of Susa. He thereby enriched forgers with another of their favorite resources, the claim to have consulted far-off official documents, preferably in an obscure language.[4]

In the fifth and fourth centuries B.C., Greek cities produced documentary evidence in the form of public inscriptions recording their rights and possessions. Antiquaries compiled from local tradition, logical inference, and thin air full lists of their cities' early rulers, their temples' early priestesses, and their games' early victors. Historians and orators gave color and detail to their accounts of earlier history by quoting treaties and other documents in extenso. Temples supported their claims to have been honored by divine visitors and to have cured human ones by producing relics and inscriptions that explained their origin.[5] This wide range of stone documents and written copies included forgeries, such as the peace treaty between Callias and the Persians, supposedly drawn up in the mid-fifth century B.C., and inspired criticism, such as the remark of Theopompus (fourth century B.C.) that the treaty of Callias must be spurious, since it was carved in the Ionic alphabet, which the Athenians had not used until the very end of the fifth century.[6] Already, then, some writers possessed an aptitude for detecting anachronisms—an aptitude essential to anyone trying either to create a plausible document or to expose one.

In fact, some evidence from the classical period suggests that sensitivity to forgery was almost as widespread as its practice. When Thucydides insists that serious history must rest on reliable and direct oral testimony about the recent past, he reveals a sense that all written evidence was at least questionable—though the speeches that he composed for Lacedemonian envoys and Athenian statesmen have themselves, in more recent times, been stigmatized as a kind of forgery.[7]

The first real heyday of the forger and the critic, however, began in the fourth century B.C. The existing traditions of forgery blossomed anew. Cities and temples turned with renewed zeal to inventing records of their heroic pasts; the temple chronicle of Lindos, compiled—supposedly from far more ancient records—in 99 B.C., with its list of donations including a vessel of unknown material left by one Lindos, the city's eponym, is only one famous example.[8] Literary forgery flourished as well, since literary traditions were transformed in Hellenistic times in ways favorable to the production of good fakes. By then the principle had been established that a literary work was the product of a specific individual with a distinctive style and set of concerns. A loose canon of classic texts in prose and verse had also begun to take shape, one which identified the most excellent writers in each genre as models for imitation. The rhetoric schools trained their pupils to turn out excellent pastiches of earlier writers, especially in the form of private letters, a favorite exercise. These could easily be taken as genuine once they came into circulation.[9] And gradually the demand for texts from this canon—real works by the individuals singled out for special admiration—outgrew the available supply.

New institutions of learning apparently intensified the demand more than the existing book market could have. In the third and second centuries B.C. the Hellenistic dynasties of the Ptolemies and the Attalids established libraries, at Alexandria and Pergamum respectively. The Ptolemies' Alexandrian library appointed poet-scholars to its staff, who assembled, collated, and imitated in their own verses the classics of older Greek literature. These gentlemen soon became known for their erudition, their zest for new material, and their many vicious arguments; as Timon of Phlius put it, writing as early as 230 B.C., "in populous Egypt they fatten up many bookish pedants who quarrel unceasingly in the Muses' birdcage."[10] The new libraries were rich, vulgar, and aggressive; they collected hundreds of thousands of the papyrus rolls on which Greek books were written. They paid especially high prices for unusually valuable texts, like the official Athenian text of the three great tragedians, Aeschylus, Sophocles, and Euripides, which the Alexandrian library borrowed against payment of a huge deposit, only to forfeit the deposit in order to keep the original rolls.[11]

The Athenian book market in the fourth century B.C. had already seen dubious orations and plays begin to drive out genuine literary currency. But the new, refined demand for rare items naturally provoked the deliberate creation by forgery of a self-renewing supply.[12] Vast numbers of faked texts accompanied the genuine ones into the libraries; spurious tragedies infiltrated the collections of Aeschylus and Sophocles, while spurious prose works clung like barnacles to the genuine ones of Plato, Hippocrates, and Aristotle. The scholars, headed by that patron of all later librarians, Callimachus, fought back. They apparently did not excise the texts they condemned as fakes from the canons. But they drew up lists (*pinakes*) of the genuine works of each major author, and identified the spurious ones as well.[13]

Though only remnants of these critical manuals, the ancestors of modern library catalogues and literary histories, survive, these show that their authors distinguished clearly between the genuine and the forged. Genuine works of a writer they classified as *gnesioi* (legitimate), the same term applied to legitimate children; spurious ones were *nothoi* (bastards); thus the ancient *Katalogos* of the works of Aeschylus includes *Aitnaiai gnesioi* and *Aitnaiai nothoi*. Genuine writing, in short, had for them an organic relation to the writer who produced it—and that relationship distinguished it from forged writing, even though the latter might be retained in libraries and lists.[14] And they used a variety of tests to identify spurious texts.

Sometimes they simply took the word of the booksellers who had assembled the corpora they collected.[15] But they also assessed the style and substance of individual works: the author of the ancient *hypothesis* or introduction to the *Rhesus*, for example, remarks that the style seems more like that of Sophocles than of Euripides, but then assigns the text to Euripides because its "pedantic concern with astronomy seems appropriate to Euripides."[16]

Early forgery thus produced historical records of a fairly distant, often heroic, past and literary remains of a canonical nature. Its existence, and its implications for the true value of high-priced acquisitions, rather than more abstract concerns, drove the scholars to make and hone weapons against it. And despite the critics it flourished mightily, both in the Greek world and—after Greek literary forms and grammatical, or scholarly, skills were transplanted to Latin soil—in Rome as well. The polymaths of later republican and early imperial Rome also confronted vast arrays of texts that needed to be judged and classified. In Rome too experts flourished, like the friend of Cicero who became known for his ability to pronounce that "this is a verse by Plautus"; "this is not." And here as well the bad currency of the forgers threatened to drive out the good; of the 130 plays of Plautus in circulation, the scholar Varro judged 109 to be forged and 21 genuine, while another canon included 25.[17]

But the Hellenistic world saw more than the persistence of ordinary literary and historical forgery. A second elaborate form flourished alongside it, one that vastly complicated the traditions with which scholars dealt and enlarged the range of tools they applied.

CHAPTER 1

Greece had long had loose groups and formal sects, the members of which tried to live by authoritative texts ascribed to legendary or very ancient founders: for example, the Orphics and the Pythagoreans. In the Hellenistic world, formerly independent Near Eastern peoples came under the rule of Alexander and his successors, kings whose language and culture were Greek. Babylonian and Egyptian priests set out to demonstrate in Greek the superior antiquity of their realms and religions. Religious leaders, inspired by patriotic feeling though rarely endowed with a deep knowledge of genuine Babylonian or Egyptian culture, tried to preserve their traditions by giving them Greek settings, and Greek texts, that claimed to come from their oldest native gods and prophets. Jews, many of whom spoke Greek, used a Greek text of the Bible and hoped to convert non-Jews to their faith and observances. They tried to prove that the Hebrew Bible was older than, and its monotheistic revelation the source of, Greek philosophy. Those who used the Greek text also tried to show that it deserved more credence than the Hebrew original from which it sometimes diverged. The members of pagan philosophical sects— Epicurean, Pythagorean, Zoroastrian—now had to offer revelations as ancient and eloquent as the Near Eastern ones. Christians, finally, had to struggle for spiritual and intellectual authority both with all of these non-Christian rivals and with Christians of divergent custom and dogma.

In this world of competing traditions and revelations, documentary authority of apparently sacred character became clothed with a glamor it had lacked in Greece in

14

earlier times. A revelation of sufficient age, authority, and historical distance could seem to be the genuine commands and teachings of a divinity. A text written in the first person and ascribed to a divine figure, one of his human companions, or an authoritative interpreter of his teachings carried a powerful guarantee of the importance and validity of its contents—one that no text by an ordinary author could rival.[18] It could offer a detailed pattern for worship and day-to-day conduct alike, thus carrying out a variety of functions that no epic, tragedy, or historical inscription could fulfill. Forgeries of this kind abounded, and the methods used to detect them grew in sophistication as the complexity of the forgeries became ever more baroque.

One classic artifact of forgery in this new key is the *Letter of Aristeas*, a long prose work probably composed in the second century B.C. It purports to explain the origin of the Greek Old Testament or Septuagint. Demetrius of Phalerum, the librarian of Ptolemy Philadelphus, ruler of Egypt early in the third century B.C., writes a memorandum to his king about acquisitions policy. He points out that the library lacks the "Books of the Laws of the Jews" and that the Hebrew texts of these, the only ones available, are inaccurate because they have never received "royal attention"—that is, because they are carelessly made personal copies, not the critically prepared and edited official copies of the Alexandrian library.[19] Demetrius receives permission to ask the high priest Eleazar to send six representatives from each of the twelve tribes to prepare a perfect, official translation. The work proceeds to defend the philosophical profundity of the elaborate Jewish ritual code and to offer instructions for good princely conduct. It concludes with the acceptance of the new translation by the Jews of Alexandria.[20]

Aristeas' letter is certainly a forgery; it begins with a gross error, the identification of Demetrius of Phalerum as Alexandrian librarian (a post he never held) under Ptolemy Philadelphus (who disliked him), and contains many other errors as well.[21] But it shows a self-consciousness and maturity of technique not encountered in previous literary fakes. The author, in the first place, uses the methods that the Alexandrian critics had developed to correct texts and detect fakes in order to make his own fake seem credible. He uses the method of allegorical exegesis—which Pergamene scholars had used to deal with what seemed to them tasteless and primitive parts of Homer, and which he perhaps encountered in the work of Alexandrian sympathizers with this method, like Apollodorus—to explain away the apparently tasteless and primitive dietary rules of Jewish tradition. He even uses the terms of textual criticism—the art of establishing correct texts by collation of manuscripts and emendation, devised by the Alexandrian scholars—to suggest the superior accuracy of the Septuagint and to undergird the credibility of his narrative.[22] And he bolsters the authority of his account by using other techniques that show a considerable knowledge of scholarly standards. Instead of telling the story of Demetrius' and Ptolemy's negotiations in his own words, he quotes Demetrius' memorandum verbatim, using the apparently genuine archival document to adorn what might otherwise seem a bare and unconvincing narrative.[23]

The author's sophistication also emerges from the literary form of his book. He writes for two audiences at once. On the one hand, he tries to show his fellow Jews that the Greek Bible used in Alexandria is superior to the Hebrew Bible of Palestine; on the other, he tries to show his non-Jewish readers that the Jewish ritual law is not a mind-bogglingly trivial and complex set of meaningless commands but an allegorical code for philosophical statements about the need for believers to pursue righteousness at all times. The work was written not for personal gain but for spiritual authority; it sought this by enfolding forgery within forgery, lie within lie, like Russian dolls in order of size. No *Parthenopaeus* could rival Aristeas' letter in complexity of design or coherence of execution.

Aristeas' forgery is perhaps the most complex spurious authority to survive, but it is only one member of a populous set. The early Christians produced them by the dozen; both the pastoral epistles to Timothy and Titus in the New Testament and numerous documents outside it, such as the *Apostolic Constitutions*, tried to settle disputes about doctrines and practices by invoking the authority of the earliest and truest Christians, speaking in the first person.[24] The fact that Near Eastern religious teachings were originally couched in difficult languages—and the associated fact that Greeks, those Americans of the ancient world, dealt with the existence of foreigners and foreign tongues by speaking Greek louder when abroad—made it particularly easy for non-Greeks in search of authority to enhance the value of their wares.[25] They claimed that what seemed trivial or obscure in Greek was merely an inadequate translation

17

from an original couched in an inaccessible holy language. Thus the author of the revelations of the Egyptian demigod Hermes Trismegistus—a member of a small patriotic sect, writing in Greek for Greek readers—explained that "when the Greeks would translate" his hieroglyphic revelations in the future, they would lose their original force and resemble ordinary, insipid Greek philosophy. He thus supported his pretense to be writing a genuinely "Egyptian" text, making a patchwork of Greek philosophical tags and poorly-understood Egyptian traditions seem both older and more alien.[26] Philo of Byblos did much the same for his own partially genuine and partially faked Phoenician histories.[27]

Between the first century B.C. and the third A.D., in short, the scholar confronted a mass of forgeries, some purporting to come from the Greek literary tradition that anyone with a good education could control, others from foreign environments about which Greeks scholars knew almost nothing precise. Some were produced simply for gain, others to support or refute complex philosophical and religious doctrines. And as one might expect, the methods used to forge works by religious and philosophical authorities infiltrated imaginative literature and other forms of extended narrative as well. The claim to derive from earlier texts written in mysterious languages and stored in mysterious places, for example, crops up in the Greek novel about the Trojan War ascribed to Dictys the Cretan.[28] The massive provision of faked documents is one of the many sophisticated elements of that greatest of late antique literary forgeries, the long and entertaining historical work now known as the *Scriptores historiae Augustae* (fourth century). Flavius Vopiscus, one of the six supposed authors of this work actually composed by one "rogue scholar," even gave the shelf-mark of one nonexistent text, the "ivory book" containing a senatus consultum signed by the emperor Tacitus. It was in bookcase 6 at the Ulpian Library, where the "linen books" containing the deeds of Aurelian were also housed.[29] Nothing could have done more to enhance the credibility of this dedicated but self-mocking imaginary scholar, whose curiosity embraced even the smallest details of imperial lives and works— and who ironically represented himself as admitting to Junius Tiberianus, the prefect of Rome, that "there is no writer, at least in the realm of history, who has not made some false statement."[30]

The pervasiveness of sophisticated forgery and the concomitant need for acute criticism are clear from the experience of some of the prolific and cultured literary men of the early Christian era. The medical writer Galen, himself a textual critic of formidable competence, saw a forged work of his own, entitled "Galen Physician," on sale in the booksellers' district of Rome, and felt impelled to write a whole book distinguishing his genuine works from the wholly and partly falsified ones that circulated under his name.[31] The satirist Lucian showed off his forger's dexterity and his critic's competence at one and the same time by forging a work in so convincing a replica of the notoriously obscure style of Heraclitus that it deceived a famous critic.[32] And Galen, who wrote elaborate text-critical and medical commentaries on many of the works ascribed to Hippocrates, frequently showed his awareness of the presence of forged passages and whole works. His commentary on the Hippocratic work *On the Nature of Man*, for example, notes that earlier commentators had condemned the work as not by Hippocrates, and that Dioscurides had marked a single passage as spurious. Galen systematically argues that the first part of the work must certainly be ancient and genuine, since Plato had already referred to it in the *Phaedrus*.[33] And he shows that the last part must certainly be late and forged, since it contains technical terms (like *sunochos* 'unbroken' and *ouremata* 'urines') which Hippocrates and other ancient doctors never used. "Those words," Galen concludes, "must come from recent doctors who did not know the ancient style."[34] No one could ask for a more systematic or cogent assessment of the authenticity of a complex text—or reveal a sharper nose for the anachronisms that reveal a late origin.[35] Galen saw the ability to identify a style as the best possible evidence that a scholar had a really solid literary foundation; when a bystander looked at the forged *Galen Physician* in Rome and threw it aside at once as an obvious fake, Galen observed that this was clearly a well-educated man.

Texts that claimed to come from outside the Greek world, however, sometimes posed more difficult analytical problems. A Greek-speaker like Dionysius of Alexandria could easily see that the same man could not have written the "flawless" Greek of the Gospel of John and the "barbarous idioms" and "solecisms" of Revelation.[36] But how could a Greek-speaker control what claimed to be translations? The classical tradition in scholarship offered no help here. Yet by early in the third century pagans and Christians alike had developed novel, clever, and still plausible tests for whether a Greek text could derive from a non-Greek original.

Julius Africanus, Christian scholar and Roman librarian, wrote a devastating letter to Origen about the story of Susanna and the elders which appears at the outset of the Greek—but not the Hebrew—text of the Book of Daniel. He thought it inauthentic for several reasons: the Jews it portrayed seemed to enjoy more freedom than was consistent with the real conditions of the Babylonian captivity, and the Daniel of the story, unlike the real prophet Daniel, prophesied in direct speech instead of by angelically inspired visions. The story as a whole, he acutely remarked, was too silly to be a Greek mime. But his chief argument was as simple as it was definitive. The story contains two crucial, elaborate puns—*in Greek*. Therefore it could not be a straight translation from the Hebrew, in which the puns would have been meaningless.[37]

Similar arguments could establish the authenticity of other segments of the canon. Jerome, whose judgments on the authenticity of several of the Epistles, first recorded in his biographies of their authors, found wide diffusion in the Middle Ages in manuscripts of the Vulgate, knew that Paul's Epistle to the Hebrews "is believed not to be his, because of its divergent style and diction." He thought that problems of translation might explain the apparent inconsistency: "Himself a Hebrew, he had written fluently in Hebrew, his own language; in consequence, what had been eloquently written in the

Hebrew was rendered more eloquently into Greek. This they allege to be the reason why the Epistle is seemingly different from the other epistles of Paul."[38]

As high classical culture gradually declined, authenticity continued to preoccupy scholars and forgery continued to attract writers. The critical tools of the grammarians remained in limited use in centers of learning. In the Greek East, for example, controversy flared occasionally around the corpus of Neoplatonic writings that were claimed to be by Dionysius the Areopagite, the Athenian convert of the Apostle Paul. One Theodore, known only from a later summary of his work, argued in the sixth century against the sophisticated view that the work must be forged, since it was not cited by the fathers of the church, did not figure in Eusebius' lists of the writings of the fathers, treated in detail ecclesiastical traditions "which grew up in the Church long after the death of the great Dionysius," and even mentioned Ignatius of Antioch, who died under Trajan, more than half a century after the time of the Apostles.[39]

Even in the Latin West, where ancient scholarship survived in more dilute form, the higher criticism was occasionally practiced. The *Hypomnesticon* attributed to Saint Augustine, for example, became the object of a massive and intelligent controversy in the ninth century. Hincmar of Reims cited the work as authentic. Prudentius of Troyes then urged its inauthenticity, pointing to its absence from Augustine's own commentary on his early work, the *Retractationes*, and its divergences from Augustine in style and content. A second theologian went even further, pointing out in the *Liber de tribus epistulis* that the work employed such non-Augustinian usages as quoting Jerome's version of the Hebrew Bible, and explaining how easily a book that dealt with matters dear to Augustine, drew on his works, and very likely presented itself as a digest of his views, could have been assigned to his authorship after his death. Hincmar ably defended the work, pointing out that Augustine had omitted mention of other clearly genuine works.[40] On the whole, to be sure, doctrinal rather than historical considerations remained decisive for most Christian scholars.[41]

Serious forgery continued to flourish during the Middle Ages. When the new nations of the High and later Middle Ages needed to support their sense of national identity by providing themselves with suitably noble pasts, they invented with abandon. The British history of Geoffrey of Monmouth, supposedly drawn from an old book in the vernacular (perhaps Welsh or Breton) in the possession of a learned friend of Geoffrey's, was only one effort to fill by imagination the gaps that separated the heroic Trojans of medieval epic and legend from their noble descendants in France, England, and elsewhere. This tradition was to last until the very end of the Middle Ages, when Johannes Trithemius, himself a notable creator of mythical texts and rulers, complained that everyone was trying to find himself a Trojan ancestor, "as if there were no peoples in Europe before the fall of Troy, and as if the Trojans included no rascals."[42] Meanwhile medieval poets and prose writers produced a vast amount of literature after the manner of such standard authors as Ovid, some of which, often by virtue of being included in one manuscript with genuine works, took on the authors' names as well. But here we confront not forgeries but pseudepigrapha—works wrongly ascribed but not intentionally deceptive.[43]

If literary and religious forgery and their counterpart modes of criticism survived the fall of the ancient world, however, forgery and criticism of legal authorities became the dominant new forms in the Middle Ages. Most practitioners of forgery and criticism were clerics and lawyers. Forgers usually wanted to equip a person or an institution with a basis for possession of lands or privileges. Their methods usually centered not on the production of literary texts—though these were written, especially when a religious order needed to justify its possession of the wonder-working bones of a saint by providing a narrative of their passage from their original home—but on the devising of faked documents, documents apparently legitimate in physical form, color, seals, and wording. As in antiquity, so in the Middle Ages, techniques of authentication could infiltrate literature. The most literary and elaborate of medieval forgeries—the *Donation of Constantine*, the notorious eighth-century document that tells the tale of how the Emperor Constantine, cured of leprosy by Pope Sylvester, showed his gratitude by conveying the entire Western empire to the Church and departing for Byzantium—makes a powerful effort to give the appearance of including legal documents formalized in expression and attested by the requisite witnesses. The volume of this activity was never small; perhaps half the legal documents we possess from Merovingian times, and perhaps two-thirds of all documents issued to ecclesiastics before A.D. 1100, are fakes. And the volume swelled enormously as scientific jurisprudence established itself firmly in the West, and every practice and possession needed written documentation; the basic code of canon law, Gratian's *Decretum*, contains some five hundred forged legal texts.[44]

In the Middle Ages as in antiquity, forgery provoked criticism. Canon lawyers became specialists in detecting fakes, and the rules they elaborated for verifying the verbal form, physical appearance, and seals of legal documents appeared beside the fakes in the *Decretum*. Some lawyers, like Pope Innocent III, became renowned for their ability to pronounce, on inspecting a document and its seals, "This is authentic"—though in the one recorded case when Innocent did so, he was wrong.[45] By the fifteenth century, courts and lawyers had accepted standards for establishing the *fides*, or credibility, of documents and narratives—to be sure, standards chiefly of an external kind. Thus in a famous lawsuit between the monks of Saint-Denis and the canons of Notre Dame, which centered on the question of which of them possessed which bits of Saint Denis himself, the lawyer for the monks insisted that his side should prevail. His position was supported by a document, the *Grandes chroniques de France*, no mere individual's account but an "approved and authorized" history preserved in a "public archive."[46]

We have moved away from the literary forgery and criticism which mainly concern us, but with the arrival of the Renaissance these return to center stage. The humanist intellectuals of fourteenth- and fifteenth-century Italy and the fifteenth- and sixteenth-century North turned back to the vast runs of material remains and literary texts which medieval scholarship had, so they thought, ignored or corrupted. They rediscovered, recopied, and

commented on literary works that medieval scholars had
known only in part or not at all, like the histories of Livy
and the poems of Catullus. They pursued and deciphered
the thousands of epitaphs and other texts that Roman
governments and Greek and Roman rulers had inscribed
on monuments and coins. And they assembled, first in
manuscript and then in print, critical editions and corpora of this new material. The ancient world suddenly
returned to solidity and life.[47]

This flood of new texts and information, however,
was heavily polluted by streams of fraudulent matter.
The new forgery stemmed less from practical needs than
from nostalgia. It aimed above all at recreating a past
even more to the taste of modern readers and scholars
than was the real antiquity uncovered by technical scholarship. Many of the early recorders of monuments and
inscriptions filled in missing texts in their notebooks just
as they would the missing limbs and heads of statues,
moved by an exuberant desire to see the ruined past
made whole again; others, still less scrupulous, supplied
whole new texts.[48] The artfulness of these could be as
refined as the emotions that inspired them were deep.
Consider, for example, the epitaph that turned up in
1485, when the body of a young Roman girl, beautifully preserved, was discovered in the Appian Way: "To
Tulliola, his only daughter, who never erred except in
dying, this monument was raised by her unhappy father
Cicero." This memento of the love and sorrow of the
great republican statesman would be even more touching
if it were not known that the neatly turned central
phrase, "quae nunquam peccavit nisi quod mortua fuit,"
was derived from another, genuine text—and that other

1 *Romae in arca aerea repertum.*

NVMA. POMPILIVS
PER. GRATIAM. DEAE. AEGERIAE
REX. S. P. Q. R
PERFECTAM. RELIGIONEM. EXOPTANS
LEGES. VBIQ. TERRARVM. INQVIRENS
AD. IVSTE. SANCTEQ. VIVENDVM
ORATORES. QVAMPLVRIMOS. MISIT
PER. VNIVERSVM. ORBEM. EVROPAM
ASIAM. AFRICAM. VT. NOMINVM
QVORVMCVNQVE. MORES. LEGES
STATVTA. CONDITIONES. PERBELLE
NOSSENT
TANDEM. HOMINES. IN. EXTREMO
BALEAR. SITV. NACTI. SVNT. PROBISS
VITAM. AGENTES. PHILOSOPHIAE
ADDICTOS. GRAECE. LOQVENTES. IN
MARIS. CONFINIO. ANTRA. DELIGENTES
PRO. DOMIBVS. PANNOSIS. VESTIBVS
INDVTOS. PARCISSIME. VICTITANTES
ARBORVM. QVIBVSDAM. FOLIIS. SCRI
BENTES. QVORVM. LEGES. CETERI
OBSERVENT..............
. . . .

Ex Michaele Scrinio.

3 *Cesenae ad secundum lapidem, in ripa Rubiconis.*
Decretum Senatus.
Vide Licet de Lucern. lib. vi. c. 2. reiicit Aug. dial. xi. 227.

IVSSV. MANDATVVE. P. R. COS
IMP. MILI. TYRO. COMILITO
MANIPVLARISVOE. CENT. TVR
MAEVAE. LEGIONARIAE. ARMAT
QVISQVIS. ES. HIC. SISTITO. VE
XILLVM. SINITO. NEC. CITRA
HVNC. AMNEM. RVBICONEM
SIGNA. ARMA. DVCTVM. CO
MEATVM. EXERCITVMNE. TR fic
ADVCITO. SI. QVIS. HIVSSCE
IVSSIONIS. ERGO. ADVERSVS
IERIT. FECERITVE. ADIVDICAT
VS. ESTO. HOSTIS. P. R. AC. SI. CO
NTRA. PATRIAM. ARMA. TVLER
IT. SACROSQVE. PENATES. E. PEN
ETRALIBVS. ASPORTAVERIT. SA
NCTIO. PLEBISCI. SENATVS
VE. CONSVLTI. VLTRA. HOS. FI
NES. ARMA. PROFERRE. LICEAT
NEMINI
S . P . Q . R

Ex Aldo & mf. Smetii.

7 *Romae animae Caesaris, id est Cometae subscriptio adjecta si-*
mulachro Divi Caesaris per Octavianum Aug. quod si-
mulachrum omnium est vetustissimum.

IPSIS LVDORVM MEORVM DIEBVS
SYDVS CRINITVM PER VII. DIES
IN REGIONE CELI SVB SEPTEM
TRIONIB. EST CONSPECTVM

Ex Apiano.

2 *Polae in Dalmatia.*
Deridet Aug. Dial. xi. p. 231.

ALEXANDEFR. PHILIPPI. REGIS. MACEDONVM
ARCHOS. MONARCHIAE. FIGVRATVS
GRAECORVM. IMPERII. INCHOATOR
MAGNI. IOVIS. FILIVS. PER. ATANABVM
NVNCIATVS. ALLOCVTOR. BRAGMANORVM
ET. ARBORVM. SOLIS. ET. LVNAE
CONCVLCATOR. PERSARVM. AC. MEDORVM
MVNDI. DOMINVS. AB. ORTV. SOLIS. VSQVE
AD. OCCASVM. A. SEPTEMTRIONE. VSQVE
AD. MERIDIEM. ILLVSTRI. PROSAPIAE
SLAVORVM. ET. LINGVAE. EORVM. PACEM
A. NOBIS. ET. SVCCEDENTIBVS. NOBIS
QVONIAM. NOBIS. SEMPER. AFFVISTIS
IN. FIDE. VERACES. IN. ARMIS. STRENVI
COADIVTORES. NOSTRI. BELLICOSI. ET. FORTES
IDCIRCO. CONFERIMVS. VOBIS. TOTAM
PLAGAM. TERRAE. ITALIAE. ΠΟΛΛ
VT. QVI. INHABITAVERINT. SINT. SVBDITI
VESTRI. ET. VESTRI. SERVI. TESTES. AVTEM
HVIVSCE. REI. SVNT. LOGOTECTA. NOSTER
ET. ALII. PRINCIPES. XI. QVOS. NOBIS. SINE
PROLE. DECEDENTIBVS. RELINQVIMVS
NOSTROS. HEREDES. ET. TOTIVS. ORBIS

Ex Manutii Orthographia.

4 *Arimini.*

C. CAESAR
DICT
RVBICONE
SVPERATO
CIVIL. BEL
COMMILIT
SVOS. HIC
IN. FORO. AR
ADLOCVT

Ex Observationibus militaribus Simeonii.

5 *In ore ponti Euxini supra*
montem erigitur columna alta
pedes XVII. crassa octo &
semis : in basi scribitur.

CAESAR
TANTVS
ERAT. QV
OD. NVLLVS
MAIOR. IN
ORBE

E Theveti Cosmographiae libro
VIII. cap. XI.

6 *Apud Benacum.*

D . D

IMP. CAESAR. PRO. SALVTE
DIVAE. CORNELIAE. SACR
VIVENTE. M. TVLLIO. ET. L
CRASSO. ET. PETRONIO. SCE
VOLA. II. VIR
HOSPES. ERAT. CAESAR. CORNELIAE
Q. PATER

Gruterus e Verderianis.

Plate 1. Fake inscriptions recording Caesar's deeds, as assembled in the last
great Renaissance collection of inscriptions, *Inscriptiones antiquae totius
orbis romani*, ed. J. Gruter (Amsterdam, 1707).

tombs and monuments to Tulliola were discovered in other places as far from Rome as Florence and Malta. Tulliola's death scene continued to be a crowd-pleaser for at least a century. But it was far from the only ancient scene to receive modern documentation. Nostalgia stimulated rich productivity: some 10,576 of the 144,044 inscriptions in the great *Corpus* of Latin inscriptions are faked or suspect; many of them are the work of imaginative Renaissance antiquaries.[49]

Literary fakes were even more ambitious than the epigraphical ones. The scholars and intellectuals of the Renaissance included a good many forgers, whose work ranged in form and ambition from the provision of new frames for genuine nuggets of old text to the free invention of whole new pasts. None of them performed the former task more proficiently than Pierre Hamon, whose clever penmanship turned a genuine Ravenna papyrus in a strikingly unfamiliar script into the will of Julius Caesar.[50] None of them performed the latter task more creatively than the Dominican from Viterbo, Giovanni Nanni (Annius). He wrote with great seriousness on problems as diverse as the freedom of the will, the licitness of pawnshops, and the early history of Viterbo, rose to the high rank of papal theologian, and even managed to die by poisoning at the hands of Cesare Borgia, a sure sign of sanctity. Yet he faked inscriptions and texts, as we will see, with equal dexterity.[51]

If the Renaissance saw an efflorescence of pasts imagined, however, it also saw the demolition of hundreds of earlier and contemporary forgeries. One of the first triumphs of the new philology of the humanists was, of course, Lorenzo Valla's detailed demonstration that the

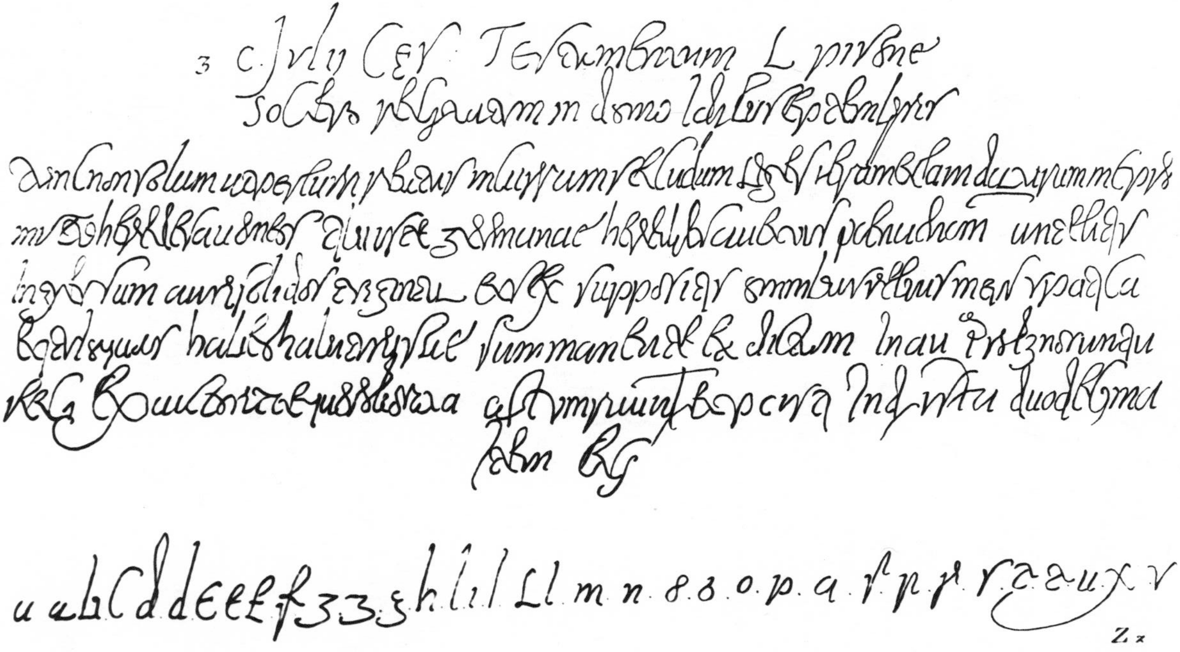

Plate 2. The will of Julius Caesar, as forged by Pierre Hamon and reproduced in facsimile in the first great handbook of the history of scripts and documents, J. Mabillon, *De re diplomatica* (Naples, 1789).

Donation of Constantine contained profuse errors of fact and phrasing that proved its medieval origin beyond doubt.[52] The Spanish jurist Antonio Agustín wrote a detailed essay, in dialogue form, on the ways of telling true inscriptions from false ones, and insisted in it that reasonable men agreed that texts should not be cited until they had been tested for genuineness and value.[53]

Moreover, the recovery of the classical heritage involved the recovery of the comments of ancient scholars on problems of authenticity. The ancient Aristotelian commentators, for example, explained that pseudepigrapha had penetrated into the Aristotelian (and other) corpora in some cases because the work in question had been written by a different author also named Aristotle; this was one of many arguments that Renaissance scholars and philosophers revived in the course of their debates about such Aristotelian texts as the *Theology* and the *De mundo*.[54] Galen, as we have seen, devoted considerable effort to identifying genuine and fake texts and portions of texts in the corpus of works attributed to Hippocrates. No wonder then that when the learned Renaissance doctor Girolamo Cardano set out to list the more valuable components of the Hippocratic canon, he used Galen's method of intensive study of diction, dialect, and style; he insisted, as a reader of Galen well might, on the difficulty of determining which texts were genuine, given that Hippocrates wrote in different genres and, presumably, at different ages. It is perhaps a little more surprising that many scholars, in the Renaissance and after, learned of Galen's views on the history of texts from his commentary on *Humors*—which was itself a Renaissance forgery.[55]

In the Renaissance, even more than in previous periods, forger and critic marched in lockstep. As professional jurisprudence spread into new areas such as the Holy Roman Empire, as professional theologians checked dogmas and practices against their supposed charters in the New Testament and elsewhere, and as a new sense of stylistic discrimination and a new historical learning reached the schools, many old forgeries were uncovered.[56] But many new ones of a more sophisticated kind were also produced, as religious orders and ruling dynasties tried to show that their age-old claims could stand up to examination, that they rested on more than merely oral tradition.

Even the most erudite of scholars occasionally fell prey to these temptations, or at least performed their tasks in ambiguous ways that led others into error. Few Renaissance scholars were more variously learned than the Hapsburg court historian Wolfgang Lazius, who used his great erudition to spectacular effect in his demonstration, supposedly based on Hebrew inscriptions found in the Vienna suburb of Gumpendorf, that the Hapsburgs were directly descended from the Hebrew leaders who settled Austria after the Flood.[57] Few were more sensitive to critical problems and methods than Joseph Scaliger, who dealt in masterly fashion with the Dionysius the Areopagite, pseudo-Phocylides, and the *Canons of the Apostles*.[58] But he also composed an anonymous Greek chronicle organized by Olympiads which many readers thought a classic, and compiled an artificial collection from the scattered verses ascribed to Astrampsychus, and thus led many readers astray, unintentionally or out of a sense of mischief.[59] And of course there were always a few—such as the sixteenth-century Simeo Bosius—who forged the sort of information that refined critics most prized, and claimed to have discovered new and excellent manuscripts of genuine, extant classical texts.[60]

In the seventeenth, eighteenth, and nineteenth centuries all these practices continued. Scholars continued to forge, sometimes in search of personal or professional gain. The Piedmontese priest Giuseppe Francesco Meyranesio contributed to the great Roman edition of Maximus of Turin, published in 1784, twenty-four new texts, supposedly drawn from manuscripts that soon disappeared in the baggage of an English milord, all in the hope of winning preferment from the edition's patron, Pius VI.[61] Sometimes the scholars forged in part for idealistic reasons, as when the Tübingen-trained theologian Christoph Matthäus Pfaff claimed to find in Turin four fragments ascribed to Irenaeus that supported his own pietist belief that the core of Christianity was the simple teachings of Christ, while "quarrels" and "schisms" arose chiefly from a misguided belief in the vital importance of particular dogmas or observances.[62]

At the same time, a new and different forgery of nostalgia grew up alongside the classical sort. National histories not fully covered in canonical texts were now filled out by the discovery of coherent documents not in the classical languages; full-blown romantic emotions not mirrored by the classics were provided with ancient inspiration of a novel sort. In the seventeenth century Curzio Inghirami's forged Etruscan texts enriched scholars' pictures of Italy's non-Roman heritage and her utopian pre-Roman past. In the eighteenth, Thomas Chat-

Plate 3. The Gothic past reinvented. A vision of Ossian's world, from J. Macpherson, *Works*, vol. 1 (Boston, 1807).

terton and James Macpherson used the traditional means—imposition of supposedly archaic script and spelling on the one hand, the claim to have translated from inaccessible originals in an unknown language on the other—to reimagine the medieval and the premedieval history of the Gothic North itself. Many early novels—*Robinson Crusoe* is only one of the most famous—that fed the new taste for close, detailed observation of human action in political or personal crisis gained the appearance of drama and veracity by representing themselves as bundles of documents discovered and assembled by objective, learned editors. So did collections of poetry. And even sophisticated reading publics, like the early readers of Horace Walpole's *Castle of Otranto*, a Gothic thriller supposedly reprinted from a black-letter original text in the library of an English recusant family, were fooled, perhaps not without complicity, by the convention.[63]

No form of serious forgery has ever entirely died. The artistic creation of supposedly historical documents has continued into the nineteenth and twentieth centuries. A. C. Buell's biography of John Paul Jones, with its documents artfully extended to make Jones seem an even greater man than he was, freeing his slaves (Cato and Scipio) after they fought bravely, is a case notorious to American historians.[64] The forgery of charters for religious belief and action was notably continued in the framing of the *Protocols of the Elders of Zion*.[65] The forgery of classical texts and objects has been practiced at a high level, as in the case of the Praeneste brooch, a golden brooch with an inscription in archaic Latin supposedly published, but in fact invented, by a German archaeologist, Wolfgang Helbig, late in the nineteenth century. It withstood criticism for more than a century before modern scientific tests and historical research established its true character.[66] And even elaborate literary texts are still forged.[67] Of necessity, modern forgers must be more technically skillful than their predecessors. But the basic techniques and topoi by which forgers evoke belief, the basic willingness of many readers and even many experts to be deceived, and the basic fact that apparently firm documents are often deeply dubious have remained unchanged. So has the rhythm by which criticism develops, demand-driven, as new ways of forging require new methods of detection. The new scientific bibliography that identifies different printing types by minute characteristics and analyzes paper chemically to date it was developed to respond to brilliant nineteenth- and twentieth-century forgers like Thomas Wise, who produced authentic-looking though previously unknown early editions of pamphlets by Elizabeth Barrett Browning and others for a vast and gullible range of collectors.[68] *Vivit fraus litteraria, et vivet.*

✳✳ 2 ✳✳

FORGERS: TYPES
AND TOOLS

FORGERY, as should by now be clear, has spread its malevolent influence through the ages. As one might expect, then, it has been provoked by circumstances and practiced by individuals of extraordinarily varied kinds. Many scholars have tried to explain its prevalence and diversity, but their general theories often oversimplify what they claim to explain. They impose clear motives and meanings on what are sometimes genuinely blurred and indecipherable situations, and assume a naïveté on the part of early writers and critics that seems unlikely in general terms and unsupported by much of the evidence.

It is often argued, for example, that forgery flourishes in cultures and periods that lack a sense of individuality, especially where writing is concerned. Forgery, like plagiarism, takes place when intellectuals do not envision genuine writing as the organic product of the author to whom it is attached. But this argument—perhaps helpful for the Middle Ages in the West, when some scholars did see repetition of what greater men had said before them as the best form of authorship—clearly does not explain Hellenistic conditions, when a keen sense of literary individuality was accompanied by a keen desire to deceive readers about authors' identities. Again, it has been argued that the prevalence of forgery, like that of pseudepigraphy in general, may simply result from the conditions of publication in a culture that lacks printed books, standard catalogues, and public libraries. This theory vaporizes on collision with the inconvenient fact that forgery has survived both the advent of printing and the rise of modern learned institutions and historical scholarship.

A final, common argument holds that early scholars simply tried to provide authorities to support doctrines and practices they considered valid, but for which they lacked written evidence or charters. But this theory, as we will repeatedly see, rests on assumptions rather than on analyzed cases of forgery. The evidence collected by Norman Cohn clearly shows that the modern forgers and supporters of the *Protocols of the Elders of Zion*— whom we can know far better than we will ever know their early counterparts—deliberately lied in what they saw as a good cause. The only reason to assume that most earlier forgers were more innocent is our own desire to explain away a disquieting feature of the past.[1]

In the end, forgery is a sort of crime. Let us then examine the three circumstances that need clarification when any crime, human or literary, is to be investigated: motive, means, and opportunity. At least it will become clear that forgery has served far too many ends for any simple thesis to tie them up in a single explanatory knot.

The motives of the forger have varied as widely as those of any other kind of creative artist. In some cases, to be sure, forgery can be tied to social or professional ambition of a simple, recognizable kind. When Ctesias set out to describe the romantic East for stay-at-home Greeks, or Nanni set out to trace the descent of the Borgias from Isis and Osiris, or Macpherson set out to show the sublimity and naive splendor of Celtic society and literature, each of them wrote as an outsider hoping to make a career. The latter two at least had their way; Nanni's ingenious fantasies won him financial support and lodging and inspired Spanish chroniclers for decades to come, and the songs of Ossian won their creator not only fame but a series of impressive jobs and pensions that transformed a poor young man forced to do literary odd jobs into a member of the social as well as the literary establishment. Even that most isolated and impoverished of forgers, Chatterton, plied his trade in the hope of preferment. The desperate sadness of his failure and suicide should not disguise him as a simple idealist; he thought that his poems, histories, and drawings of ancient Bristol could win him publication and promotion. And in at least a few cases—such as that of Helbig, creator of the Praeneste brooch—careerism seems a powerful as well as an accurate characterization of motive. Helbig made his great find while he was desperate to establish a career as an archeologist in Rome; he had been devoid of powerful support back home in Germany. The brooch not only supported his theories but made him the grey eminence of Roman archeology for many years after 1887.[2]

In other cases, however, the motives seem less materialistic, even fanciful. Dionysius and Coleman-Norton had nothing but amusement to gain from their little mystifications; the sadistic pleasure derived from seeing others fooled seems to be a prevalent form of gratification.[3]

But Schadenfreude is not the only emotional reward that has driven forgers. Consider the case of the *Acts* of Paul, one of the many noncanonical texts, often very curious, which rivaled the Gospels and Epistles we now know as the New Testament in the early centuries of Christianity, and which were normally excluded from the canon for theological rather than philological reasons. This one tells the story of how Thecla, a devout woman of pagan descent, tried to follow Paul; promised to cut her hair lest it be an occasion of desire; baptized herself and her fellow prisoners in the arena into which she was thrown; was saved by a virtuous lioness from the other wild animals there; and lived an exemplary life of Christian fortitude despite tortures and temptations. Caught and convicted of forging this supposedly apostolic document, the author admitted that his work was not only noncanonical but a deliberate fake. But he also explained that he had a reason for what he did. He composed the text out of love—love for Paul.[4] In most cases in which forgers have attributed greater deeds, more magnanimous sentiments, and more eloquent words to historical figures than the record warrants, love has probably been their preeminent motivation.[5]

Others have forged from hatred. No forger is more notorious in modern literary scholarship than John Payne Collier, a self-made man who began as a journalist in the early nineteenth century, became a great authority on the early history of English drama, and spent his last years in disgrace, after a few of his many rivals revealed that he had salted his histories and editions of texts with invented or improved documentation supposedly found in private and public libraries. None of his forgeries is more notorious than the folio Shakespeare annotated by the "Old Corrector"—an early annotator whose corrections to the transmitted text Collier thought authoritative and used in quantity in his editorial work. Collier's nineteenth-century enemies destroyed his reputation by analyzing the Old Corrector's notes, showing that some of the corrections were modern fakes, first entered in pencil and then inked in an imitation of the Old Corrector's hand. The demonstration ruined Collier's protracted later life. But in fact, as he always claimed, this particular attack on his probity was itself in part a literary crime. The actual author of these interpolated readings seems to have been not Collier but his better-educated and socially superior enemy Sir Frederick Madden, Keeper of Manuscripts in the British Museum. Madden hated Collier for a variety of reasons; he had the training and experience to carry out the forgery (and in fact his hand resembles the forger's more closely than Collier's does); and he had the volume in his custody before the decisive marks were discovered. Collier undoubtedly forged textual documents to enhance his reputation and support his theories. But in this one case at least the apparently plausible explanation based on ambition—Collier's desire to rise in the calling of literary scholarship at a time when its standards and methods were still undefined— dissolves when tested against the facts of the case and Madden's malice.[6]

Since forgeries are intellectual and scholarly projects, and often far from trivial ones, the invocation of motives and ambitions rarely explains them fully.[7] Most forgeries of any scale and depth strive not only to advance the career of their creator but to support his beliefs and opinions. Helbig's Praeneste brooch, for example, exemplified in an electrifyingly precise way his theories about what the earliest form of Latin should look like. Nanni's histories of the world discredited the increasingly popular ones of the ancient Greek writers whose influence in Italian humanist culture he deplored.[8]

The many Near Eastern-styled forgeries of the Hellenistic period and the Empire were clearly something more than mere mystifications of the credulous. Their authors sincerely believed that they were descended from races and cultures older and nobler than the victorious Greeks and Romans. They tried as systematically as they could to assemble the genuine records and practices of ancient Egypt and Babylon. But the traditional intellectual elites who had sustained and cultivated their cultures were at best in disarray, at worst dispersed and demoralized. Accordingly—like those Meso-Americans who tried to revive their native traditions of worship and divination after the Spanish conquest—they spoke not in the genuine voice of a surviving tradition still maintained but in the dilute one of the victim uprooted from a lost tradition still beloved. Philo of Byblos, Hermes Trismegistus, and pseudo-Manetho, author of the *Book of Sothis*, lied to promote what they saw as profound, forgotten truths about the cosmos and the past.[9]

Some forgers are clearly raffish individuals, irresponsible about ethical questions and standards outside as well as inside the realm of literature. Edmund Backhouse, the "Hermit of Peking," the twentieth-century English baronet who foisted his forged documents of erotic chinoiserie on historians and general readers, was hounded all his life by financial and personal scandal. A fantasist and liar, one involved in large-scale confidence tricks as well as forgery, he seems the prototypical rogue willing to corrupt anyone or anything, including his own considerable gifts as a Chinese scholar, to turn a dishonest living.[10]

Karl Benedikt Hase, one of those German émigrés who so enlivened the cultural life of early nineteenth-century Paris, seems a natural candidate to be a distorter of the historical record, as he was when he composed, edited, translated into Latin, and elaborately commented on a Greek text he claimed to have discovered in Paris, a text that seemed to be the earliest record—centuries older than any other—of Russian history. After all, he sometimes had to scratch for a living and rarely displayed keen ethical scruples. His diary, kept in fluent if occasionally unclassical Greek and preserved in the Bibliothèque Nationale, records not only his forays into restaurants for "biftek" but also his expeditions into the back streets for congress with "two prostitutes and a dildo." This characteristic figure out of Eugène Sue, creeping from flare to flare along the mysterious, filthy streets of Paris before Hausmann drove his boulevards through the stews, seems to make a natural criminal.

But Hase's case is not in fact clear or simple. He was a grave and incredibly hard working scholar, one who revealed his mastery of Greek philology not only with the Greek text of "Toparcha Gothicus," the forged Russian history that survived inspection for a century, but with a host of legitimate philological projects. He edited genuine Byzantine texts from the most crabbed and fragmentary manuscripts with skill, devotion, and unswerving attention to detail. He contributed vast amounts of material to one of the greatest of the nineteenth century's collaborative enterprises—the Didot edition, still the standard one, of Henri Estienne's *Thesaurus linguae Graecae*. He delighted Frenchmen and foreign visitors alike with the wit and learning that won him the affectionate nickname "Father Hase."[11]

Hase's reputation as man and critic has at least been mixed; that of Erasmus has been almost spotless. Modern scholars quite reasonably revere him as one of the great exposers of error and mendacity. He had a deep knowledge of ancient history and literature and a keenly discriminating sense of style. Turned on the rich corpus of texts traditionally attributed to Seneca—some classical and some late, some pseudepigraphical and some forged, and some by another author of the same name—these sharp instruments of dissection easily excised the supposed correspondence of Seneca and Saint Paul from the genuine matter. Erasmus' pungent preface used stylistic, historical, and substantive arguments: "There is nothing in the letters from Paul worthy of Paul's spirit. One hardly hears the name of Christ, which normally pervades Paul's discourse. [The author] makes that powerful defender of the Gospel cowardly and timorous. . . . And it's a sign of monumental stupidity when he makes Seneca send Paul a book *De copia verborum* [*On Building Vocabulary*] so that he will be able to write better Latin. If Paul did not know Latin he could have written in Greek. Seneca did know Greek."[12]

Purging the spurious, in fact, was central to Erasmus' sense of his calling as a Christian scholar. It inspired his removal of the *comma Johanneum* (1 John 5:7), the most explicit scriptural support for the doctrine of the

Trinity, from his first edition of the New Testament. His distaste for a culture nurtured on literary deceit emerges from his life of Jerome, with its trenchant attack on the medieval legends of superhuman cures and interventions that had distorted and disguised the facts.[13] When Erasmus defended the arguments by which he, like Lorenzo Valla before him, had denounced the corpus of Dionysius the Areopagite, he made clear his opposition to all production of fraudulent works, even in support of desirable ends: "In those days even pious men thought it pleasing to God to use this deceit to inspire the people with eagerness to read."[14]

In 1530, Erasmus published his fourth edition of the works of Saint Cyprian. This included as a stop-press supplement a treatise, *De duplici martyrio* (*On the Two Forms of Martyrdom*), which, as its table of contents said, was "discovered in an ancient library; may it be possible to search out other valuable works of his as well."[15] The treatise praised the virtues of martyrs in the traditional sense, those who died to bear witness to the truth; but it went on to praise other forms of Christian life—the life of those willing to die but not called upon to do so, the life of the virgin who struggles to avoid a sin—as equivalent in merit to martyrdom. It takes a position highly sympathetic to Erasmus, who had always disliked the kind of Christianity that equated suffering with virtue, and had always preferred the human Christ hoping to avoid death in Gethsemane to the divine Christ ransoming man by dying at Calvary. It is preserved in no known manuscript or ancient library. It explicates scriptural passages in peculiar ways, ways also found in Erasmus' New Testament commentaries. And it is written in a beautiful but peculiar Latin honeycombed with biblical and patristic citations and marked by a frequent use of nouns with diminutive endings—the very Latin in which Erasmus wrote the great literary works that he acknowledged, like *The Praise of Folly*, and the funnier one that he did not, the *Julius Excluded from Heaven*. *De duplici martyrio* is not Erasmus' discovery but his composition; it marks an effort to find the support of the early Church for his theology at the cost—which he elsewhere insisted must never be paid—of falsifying the records of that Church. The greatest patristic scholar of the sixteenth century forged a major patristic work.[16]

Erasmus was not the only grave and learned gentleman to hoax the entire world of learning with an uncharacteristic piece of fakery. Carlo Sigonio, later in the sixteenth century, was the dominant scholar of his day in two or three fields—the reconstruction of the chronology and constitutional history of early Rome, the history of medieval Italy, and the theory of historiography. A revered teacher and prolific writer, he was especially known for his mastery of Cicero's works and his own ability to write pure Ciceronian prose. Early in the 1580s he brought out a new text supposedly communicated to him by a printer—the *Consolation*, mentioned above, which Cicero wrote on his daughter's death. This work, preserved only in fragments and testimonies by classical authors, was avidly bought, eagerly read, and immediately denounced. Contemporary readers thought the work tried far too hard to prove its own authenticity; it contained Italianisms of style, alien turns of thought, and even phrases borrowed from earlier Renaissance writers. Though not all agreed where responsibility must

M. TVLLII
CICERONIS
CONSOLATIO,
VEL
De luctu minuendo.

Fragmenta eius à Carolo Sigonio,
& Andrea Patritio
expofita.

Antonij Riccoboni iudicium, quo
illam Ciceronis non effe
oftendit:

Caroli Sigonij pro eadem orationes II.

BONONIAE,
Apud Ioannem Rofsium. M D X X C I I I.
De Superiorum licentia.

Plate 4. C. Sigonio's forged *M. Tullii Ciceronis Consolatio*
(Bologna, 1593), a forgery that resembles a piece of scholarship
(cf. plate 5) minutely.

FRAGMENTA
CICERONIS,
VARIIS IN LOCIS
DISPERSA,

Caroli Sigonii diligentia collecta,
& fcholiis illuftrata
Quæ fequens pagina indicat.

VENETIIS, M. D. LIX.
Ex Officina Stellæ, Iordani Zilleti.

Plate 5. C. Sigonio's *Fragmenta Cicececeronis* (Venice, 1559), a
collection of the real fragments of Cicero.

lie, many attached it to Sigonio himself, especially when he defended the book, lamely but doggedly, against all attackers. The controversy brought only discredit on Sigonio, and the text itself seems unworthy of his attention, or his authorship.[17] Still, it seems certain that Sigonio did write it, perhaps as an exercise in the rhetorical genre of the *Consolation*, perhaps with help—yet certainly under false pretenses. In this case as in Erasmus', a great scholar emerges as a great sinner against the elementary rules of scholarship, even though nothing in his earlier life prepares us for this. In Sigorio's case, unlike in Erasmus', there is no obvious idealistic justification for his act.

The desire to forge, in other words, can infect almost anyone: the learned as well as the ignorant, the honest person as well as the rogue. In some contexts, naturally, it did not seem so immoral as in others—or, perhaps, did not seem immoral at all. Nanni, for example, was a Dominican; the mendicant friars of the later Middle Ages often seem to have acted on the assumption that real records and facts needed to be heightened and dramatized if they were to do justice to their sacred subjects. Medieval Dominican biographers of Saint Jerome embroidered the facts they had with the more colorful story that he had reappeared again and again after his death in solid, material form—that he had pushed an insufficiently respectful abbot to the edge of a cliff and allowed him to live only after he promised to build a church and dedicate it to Jerome. Early sixteenth-century Dominicans in Bern adorned a statue of the Virgin Mary with drops of varnish, to show that the statue wept and thus possessed miraculous powers; they even spoke through her lips, in-

serting a speaking tube to utter supposedly divine prophecies and commands.[18] Like those earlier rabbis whose
exegetical method of *aggadah*, the provision of edifying
stories, filled in the factual gaps and missing motives in
the austere dramas of the Pentateuch, the Dominicans
invented the texts and facts they needed even when dis-
cussing subjects and beings of the utmost seriousness.
There was after all no other way, in this increasingly lit-
erate and critical age, to defend the orally transmitted
traditions of the late medieval church. Nanni partici-
pated not only in a long-term literary tradition of forgery
but in the late medieval fiction-producing culture of his
order as well; no wonder, then, that he felt licensed to
restore the truth by *pia fraus*.

But to infer, as some historians have done, from single
cases like Nanni's the more general assertion that the
flourishing of forgery reveals that early periods did not
share our notion of truth and authority, is surely unjusti-
fied. Forgery evidently tempts the virtuous as well as the
weak, and has been practiced by those who condemned
it most sharply. General theses cannot possibly do justice
to this tangle of complex individual cases.

If generalizations shed little light on the obscure realm
of ends, they brilliantly illuminate the vivid realm of
means. Forgers have been as consistent over the ages in
their choice of media as they have been diverse in their
personalities and interests. A relatively restricted group
of colors makes the forger's palette, now as two millennia ago. After all, the forger has to carry out a limited
range of tasks, one that has not altered greatly over time.
He must give his text the appearance—the linguistic appearance as a text and the physical appearance as a docu-

ment—of something from a period dramatically earlier than and different from his own. He must, in other words, imagine two things: what a text would have looked like *when it was written* and what it should look like *now that he has found it.* Two forms of imagination should lead to two different, complementary acts of falsification: he must produce a text that seems distant from the present day and an object that seems distant from its purported time of origin. Two further technical tasks remain: he must explain where his document came from and reveal how it fits into the jigsaw puzzle of other surviving documents that makes up his own period's record of an authoritative or attractive period in the past. Imagination and corroboration, the creation of the forgery and the provision of its pedigree: these deceptively simple requirements are almost all that a forger has to meet. But they are not exhaustive, and the last one is as crucial as it is often elusive. The forger needs to give his work an air of conviction and reality, a sense of authenticity. Just as a man applying for a substantial loan will enter his bank with shined shoes, pressed pants, and a vest with white piping on its edges, so the serious forgery must go out to meet the world with the extra confidence provided by a general air of solidity and prosperity, and must distract the world from the worn spots and defects that might arouse alarm and suspicion. And in this final area, as we will see below, means are more varied and problems harder to surmount than in the others.

No forger gives more vivid instances of normal technique applied in a stimulating and original way than the eighteenth-century masters Thomas Chatterton, forger of poems, treatises, and histories purporting to derive from and describe late medieval Bristol, and William Henry Ireland, creator of artifacts and documents supposedly connected with Shakespeare, as well as a complete forged play by him, *Vortigern*. Both were young; both nonetheless managed to deceive some of the learned, if eccentric, amateur scholars and antiquaries who were in their time the practitioners of English philology. Chatterton imagined an entire physical world of grand gates, towering walls, and noble churches; he gave each of these structures a physical form in sketches and a continuous history in accompanying documents. In his texts he performed an even more difficult and striking feat of historical empathy: he assembled and employed a reconstructed language, which made use of archaic words drawn from the standard glossaries of Chaucer and other early writers, and he imposed a spelling chiefly notable for its heavy-handed use of extra consonants and unusual vocalization to create *Verfremdungseffekt*. The script was Chatterton's carefully cultivated "medieval" one; some of the many documents he produced were written on parchment and aged by dyeing (he sometimes used tea to produce a satisfying browning of page and text alike). The result evidently struck most eighteenth-century readers as several centuries old.[19]

One sample of Chatterton's work will suggest its scholarly depth, imaginative consistency, and period flavor. A short poem by W. Canynge—whom Chatterton normally described not as a poet but as the patron of a poet, Thomas Rowley, to whom he ascribed the bulk of his forgeries—calls up a sunny vision of late medieval

England, populated by many fat, somnolent worthies
and a few lean, sharp poets. It is a lyric in the vein of
Brueghel:

> THOROWE the halle the Belle han sounde
> Byelecoyle doe the Grave beseeme
> The Ealdermenne doe lye arounde
> And snoffelle oppe the cheorte steeme
> Lyke asses wylde ynne desarte waste
> Swotellye the Morneynge Ayre doe taste
> Syche coyne theie ate. the Minstrels plaie
> The tyme of Angelles doe thei kepe
> Heie stylle the Guestes ha ne to saie
> Butte nodde yer thankes ande falle aslape
> Thos echone daie bee I to deene
> Gyf Rowley Iscamm or Tyb. Gorges be ne seen.[20]

Here the language is deliberately quaint and naive, and
the spelling multiplies consonants in all directions. Chatterton wrote out the whole lyric, moreover, in an archaic
script on a parchment which also bore two coats of arms.
He thus provided a physical as well as a poetic relic of
that Bristol elite of high spirits who had longed for one
another's company among the snoring, overfed Babbitts
of the mercantile town. And Tyrwhitt, the editor of the
1777 edition of Chatterton's poems, no doubt sensed the
multiple attractions of the relic when he included an en-
graved facsimile of it along with what were otherwise
straight texts. Chatterton hoped that this document, at
once physical and textual, could impart to the whole corpus the double attraction that a forgery needs: the feeling
of alienness from its reader's present and from its own
time of origin.

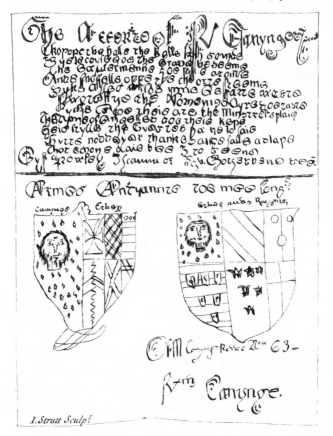

Plate 6. The forgery as *Gesamtkunstwerk*: Chatterton's forged
parchment with the poem on Canynge's Feast. From
T. Chatterton, *Poems* (London, 1777).

Students of forgery, as of other literary forms, tend to specialize in one period, and often try to tie the ruses of their particular forgers tightly to their forgers' immediate contexts. Recent students of Chatterton and Ireland, for example, have suggested that their sophisticated efforts to produce texts and objects that looked genuinely historical were connected with the larger transformation of historical studies that was taking place around them. Eighteenth-century scholars began not only to praise the deeds of kings but also to tease out the texture of everyday life in the past. They supported their narratives by detailed quotation of documents precisely identified, and concerned themselves in a serious way with the problem of historical knowledge, using more and more sophisticated techniques to check the age and watermarks of paper, the colors of ink, the forms of script, and the other external signs of validity. Chatterton's and Ireland's forgeries had to wear their heavy armor of external and internal evidence precisely because they would encounter more sophisticated criticism than their predecessors.[21]

This argument undoubtedly carries weight. But if one sets Chatterton's and Ireland's techniques into their long-term context, the tradition of Western forgery, it soon becomes clear that there was little radically new in what they did. Forgers had sought since antiquity itself to give their works the appearance of age. The notion that a forgery must use an appropriately archaic language, for example, was familiar to Nanni three centuries earlier. He entitled one of his fakes, Berosus' history of the ancient world, a *Defloratio* (a term he had found in the sixth-century Latin translation of Josephus' *Jewish*

Antiquities), and then commented in his note that "it is the custom of the orientals to call a brief narrative drawn from public authority a *Defloratio*," thus establishing the foreign character of Berosus' language (the fact that Berosus had not written in Latin but in Greek, Nanni politely ignored).[22] The notion that a good forgery should be clothed in a suitably archaic external form was also mother's milk to Nanni. He had the famous edict of the Lombard king Desiderius—an "ancient monument" which he "discovered" in a staged excavation—written in a facsimile of Lombardic script (which we now know, as he did not, to have been used only in manuscripts, not in inscriptions).[23] And he had his fake historians printed up in a splendid large Roman type no doubt meant to suggest the fonts used for the Latin Bible, and thus to convey the impression of age and authority that a really ancient priestly annalist deserved.

These techniques, moreover, were not invented but re-discovered in the fifteenth century. After all, the notion that archaic forms and an unusual script revealed the great age of a document was already familiar in Greece in the mid-fifth century. The seventh-century inscriptions Herodotus saw on tripods in Boeotian Thebes, which he thought must go back all the way to the days of Laius and Oedipus, seemed ancient and authoritative because they were written in"Cadmean letters"—in other words, an alphabet like the old Ionian one.[24]

Old forms of literary expression could also be used when new ones failed to give the desired impression. When the Jews of the Hellenistic period tried to show the organic connection between their revelation and the cul-

ture of classic Greece, they did so with ingenious direct-
ness. They simply composed verses that used the normal
language and meter of Greek tragic and epic poetry, ascribed them variously to the pagan prophetesses, or sibyls, and the great Greek writers, like Sophocles, and in-
stilled them with suitably monotheistic sentiments. They
imagined, in short, what an Athenian tragedian would
have done to express his faith in one all-powerful and
omnipresent divine being.[25] The *Historia Augusta* goes
even further in this direction, providing lashings of apparently inconsequential detail about the beliefs, say-
ings, magical practices, and sexual habits of the emperors in order to call up a three-dimensional, convincing
picture of their times—much as a genuine biographer
like Suetonius had.

Even the notion that a good forgery must be aged arti-
ficially to prove its distance from its origin was hardly
new with Nanni. It would be hard to venture a guess as
to the earliest practitioner of "distressing," as this art is
called in the theater and the antique furniture business,
but one suspects that it was as familiar in the classical
world as it was in the classical China of the fifth century,
where forgers "used drippings from thatched roofs to
change the color of the paper, and further mistreated the
paper deliberately, so that it looked like an old piece of
writing."[26] The effort to imagine the world that produced one's text and the effort to give it a patina of age
are not something new in the Enlightenment but part of
the *longue durée* of literary fraud.

The eighteenth-century forgers lavished space and
imagination on the origins and setting of their creations

as well as on their content and wording. Ireland designed and executed the myth of the aristocratic stranger from near Stratford who had befriended him and provided him with his rich stock of artifacts and manuscripts as elaborately as he did the texts themselves.[27] Chatterton too devised a story of archival discovery in a forgotten church muniment room to explain his ability to produce so many novelties. And both of them made every effort to show that their findings from these new texts could somehow be assimilated to the best scholarship of their day, even when doing so involved fast footwork, as when Chatterton mentioned a male Saint Werburgh, was informed that the saint was in fact a woman, and promptly made his supposed sources explain that the woman saint was named after the male one, who had converted her.[28]

These devices, and the concern for sophisticated cross-verification that underpins them, have also been explained as a response to new conditions of inquiry. In the seventeenth and eighteenth centuries, scholars subjected the credibility of all witnesses—even the evangelists—to searching scrutiny. The new historical criticism applied to traditional accounts of the past by Philip Cluverius, Jacob Perizonius, and Giambattista Vico rejected even the best-established traditional myths, like the Roman one of Romulus, Remus, and the wolf. The forgers naturally had to meet the new critical standards of their day; hence their profusion of authenticating technical detail. Here too, however, the eighteenth-century forgers worked within long-established traditions. Since the ancient world, forgers had felt they had to explain how they could have come across stunning novelties previously unknown. They did so just as Chatterton and Ireland would: by inventing mysterious but impressive origin stories.

When the priests of Israel claimed to have found the book of the law in the temple, or the author of the preface to the Trojan romance of Dictys the Cretan claimed to have found his text in a storage cellar at Cnossus laid open by an earthquake, or Geoffrey of Monmouth claimed to have read his Trojan legends in an old British book belonging to Archdeacon Walter, all of them provided the same sort of archival pedigree that Chatterton's muniment room offered—an apparent guarantee that what might seem an individual's free invention had in fact been preserved for uninterrupted centuries in an inviolable archive. The same topoi of impressive books suddenly appearing have long outlasted their supposed Enlightenment origins, as the history of Mormonism shows. And the same deep-seated need to believe miraculous stories of surprise discovery seems to have been at work in all cases; in any event the same tales have been received with equal warmth and credulity in a dizzying range of times, places, and cultural settings.

A second authenticating method employed by Chatterton, akin but not identical to the first, was the provision of a textual (as opposed to an archival) guarantee of authority—the provision, that is, of the name and vital circumstances of some past writer who stands as witness to the fraud. In his case at least—and it is far from unique—the authentication is complex, even doubled on itself. His chief source for medieval Bristol was (supposedly) the fifteenth-century priest Thomas Rowley, the purported author of the works Chatterton discovered.

But Rowley in turn had a chief source whom he liberally quoted, the still earlier imaginary figure whom he cited as "myne Authour Turgotte." This displacement of authority from the forged text before us to a nonexistent earlier source from which it comes can be connected to Chatterton's context; it closely resembles the methods of the epistolary novelists of the time, with their substitution of an imaginary narrator and a later editor, working as it were in dialogue with one another, for a single author's narrative voice. And it resembles the tactics of such early novelists as Defoe, well described in a classic essay by Leslie Stephen, who cover up the inconsistencies of their narrative by offering a complex account of the authorities they come from, often an account that does not really offer solid support.[29] But it also has ample precedent in the tradition. Ctesias, trumpeting his researches in the archives of Susa, would have recognized a brother in Chatterton two millennia later.

As old as the need to account for the origin of a fake is the need to fit it neatly into the ordered ranks of other sources, real, fake, and ambiguous, which readers may be expected to know. The forger confronts a chessboard full of pieces: relevant, possibly relevant, all-but-irrelevant, and genuinely irrelevant facts; corroboratory and contradictory texts. How is he to move his own new pieces in such a way as not to expose them to a rapid checkmate? Two possibilities have consistently presented themselves. The forger may claim to sweep the board clean of any pieces but his own. Or he may try to castle, using genuine pieces to intervene between his own shaky falsehoods and detection. Often he undertakes both maneuvers—contradictory though they seem—at once.

Nanni, for example, affords a splendid case of the forger who mounts a frontal attack. He knew perfectly well that his new texts could not be assimilated to the Greek ones; his account of ancient history, which attributed all creativity to Egyptians, Jews, and early Italians, and mingled the tribal leaders of medieval myth with the patriarchs of biblical history, could not be true if Herodotus and Thucydides were. Instead of denying the contradictions, however, he boldly and repeatedly affirmed them. Ranging the rhetorical spectrum from simple abuse to complex argument, he described the Greeks themselves as "dirty, fetid and goatish" and used their disagreements as evidence that they were congenital liars: "The Greeks fight and disagree with one another, as is not surprising, and they have entirely ruined history as well as philosophy with their civil war." Only his texts—which demonstrated that "the Iberians, Samotheans and Tuyscons were clearly the fathers of letters and philosophy, more than a thousand years before the Greeks"—deserved credence as the work of priestly authors who had followed archival sources.

This seems the simplest of arguments, the lie direct. Yet Nanni also employed a more devious and sinister retort courteous. Whenever possible he used the authority of and the facts recorded by the very Greeks he denounced to reinforce his imaginings. When he denounced "lying Ephorus and the dreamer Diogenes Laertius" for their belief that Greek philosophy was an independent creation, he cited Aristotle "in his Magic" for the true view—a Greek against a Greek (in fact he had learned about Aristotle's *Magic* from the very work by Diogenes that he wished to discredit).[30] When he

wove the bright myth of Isis and Osiris into the dull
tapestry of early history, he drew heavily on the Greek
compilation of Diodorus Siculus, recently made available in Latin by the humanist translator Poggio Braccio-
lini. And when he made his supposed Roman historian
Sempronius base his chronology of the Trojan War on
Eratosthenis invicta regula—"the unvanquished rule of
Eratosthenes"—he was not inventing boldly, as at least
one distinguished modern student has thought.[31] Rather,
he was quoting literally from another humanist translation, by Lampugnino Birago, of another Greek text: in
this case, the *Roman Antiquities* of Dionysius of Halicarnassus, who had declared that his own chronology rested
on the *canones* ("tables," wrongly translated as *regulae*
by Birago) of the Hellenistic scholar and scientist Eratosthenes.[32]

These moves involve some contradiction in principle,
to be sure. When read in their original form, however,
Nanni's attacks on and uses of the same writers paradoxically reinforce one another. The continual assertion of
authority and denunciation of mendacity give Nanni's
texts an air of moral as well as factual superiority. The
presence of facts and ideas, some of them quite refined,
that are shared with the recently rediscovered Greek
works reassured some readers who would have found a
total refusal to assimilate the new material cause for
worry. Nanni's intellectual cake remained undiminished,
no matter how greedily he ate it. And in this case too,
Nanni was no exception but an instance of a general
rule. Almost every other large-scale forger known to us,
from Ctesias in antiquity to such crude and incompetent
modern epigones as Kujau, has inserted as much attested

fact as possible into his creations to give the pure fantasies ballast and structure. The most ambitious forger
imaginable, then, the one who seeks to reorient his contemporaries' mental maps of a whole sector of the past,
must apparently depict many familiar landmarks even
when he insists that he is not doing so. And most literary
forgery, like artistic forgery, is not creation from whole
cloth but the production of free imitation, close pastiche,
or a rococo frame to set off genuine fragments in a new
way. Nothing else would make sense or carry conviction.[33]

Structural techniques like these are necessary but not
sufficient to the creation of a successful forgery. One further effort, as amorphous as it is important, must still be
made: the creation of an air of verisimilitude and signifi-
cance. In this effort as opposed to the others we have so
far surveyed, forgers' tactics have varied as widely as the
contexts they worked in and the audiences they hoped to
impress. But some long-lived favorite techniques can be
identified. Apparently casual verbal details, dropped as
though inadvertently into a larger passage, are used to
make the larger whole convincingly antique. Thus the
author of Book 16 of the *Corpus Hermeticum* not only
dismisses the Greek translation of his tract as necessarily
inadequate but makes plain that he is an ancient Egyptian prophesying what will happen in the distant future.
And he does so by the simple expedient of adding an
adverb: when the Greeks translate his words *husteron*—
"later on"—he says, their efforts will be in vain. This
elegant turn greatly amused Isaac Casaubon, the great
unmasker of the *Corpus*. "*Husteron*," he wrote in the

margin of his copy; "my, what a lover of drama it was who wrote this."[34]

Neither the gesture nor its eventual loss of power to convince was unique. Dictys the Cretan made a similar, and to the modern reader even more blatant, effort to show that he was a very ancient writer indeed. At the end of Book 5 he carefully explained that he had written in the Punic (Phoenician) script introduced by Cadmus and Danaus, and in the mixed dialect typical of Cretans. The great seventeenth-century scholar Jacob Perizonius found it all too easy to point out that no writer would really explain that he was using the script and language normal for his time and place: "What need was there to tell his contemporaries—the ones whom writers chiefly have in mind—that he used the only script then known? Would it not seem ridiculous to tell one's readers today that one had had his book published by printing it, using the technique invented 250 years ago? I think it is now patently clear that these suggestions were made for the benefit not of the men of the Trojan period but for those who lived in the time of Nero, centuries later."[35]

If the subtle detail that suggests has been the chief internal, or textual, way to win respect for fakes, the blare of publicity and rant of rhetoric have been the chief external ones. Surprisingly few forgers try to slip their wares cautiously past the guardians of the canon. On the contrary, they have often tried to make as great a splash as possible. When Nanni decided to challenge Greek historiography, he assembled his texts and commentaries in a single massive volume, splendidly printed and adorned with a nostalgic illustration of the true form of early

Plate 7. The forger as recreator of a vanished world. Nanni's vision of ancient Rome, from G. Nanni, *Antiquitates* (Rome, 1492).

Rome. Similarly, when the Hermit of Peking set out to rewrite the modern history of China, he did so by inter-polating translations of his fakes into works written for a very large public—and by donating hundreds of scrolls of unequal value to the Bodleian Library.

Noise, light, and publicity—accompanied by the references we have learned to expect to books that fall from the sky and leap from ditches—normally accompany the birth of a grand fake. As these cases suggest, one element of the crime of forgery that has altered surprisingly little over time is opportunity. One would expect the rise of fixed libraries, reference books, and catalogues, and the increasing numbers of professional literary and bibliog-raphical scholars who produce them, to have reduced the chances of pulling off a forgery of a major text to nil. In fact, however, these changes in the environment have re-duced the chances of success only for unskilled forgers who cannot slip their works past more sensitive instru-ments of detection. The forger with imagination is only stimulated to new heights of enterprise by conditions that one would expect to put him out of business. And even now, collectors and librarians fascinated by a single writer or type of text often forget (until too late) to apply basic physical and bibliographical tests that could pro-tect them from others' deceptions.

One who studies the career of forgery in the West may well wonder if the human mind nourishes a deep-seated desire to be taken in as grandly and thoroughly as pos-sible. *Muntus fuld tezibi*—"the world wants to be fooled"—is after all the motto on the title page of one of the greatest of all exposés of scholars' propensity to be fooled, J. B. Mencke's orations *On the Charlatanry of*

Plate 8. The world of the learned portrayed as a theater in which the audience of scholars shows itself not critical but gullible; J. B. Mencke, *De la charlatanerie des savans* (The Hague, 1721), frontispiece.

the Learned.[36] Such hypotheses are too grand for historians. But one small regularity may be observed. If any law holds for all forgery, it is quite simply that any forger, however deft, imprints the pattern and texture of his own period's life, thought, and language on the past he hopes to make seem real and vivid. But the very details he deploys, however deeply they impress his immediate public, will eventually make his trickery stand out in bold relief, when they are observed by later readers who will recognize the forger's period superimposed on the forgery's. Nothing becomes obsolete like a period vision of an older period.

We all know this phenomenon in another artistic context. Hearing a mother in a historical movie of the 1940s call out "Ludwig! Ludwig van Beethoven! Come in and practice your piano now!" we are jerked from our suspension of disbelief by what was intended as a means of reinforcing it, and plunged directly into the American bourgeois world of the filmmaker. Forgery illustrates the same principle continually and beautifully. The passages from Hermes and Dictys that irked Casaubon and Perizonius make good cases in point.

An even better case is offered by a supposedly ancient vase published in the early nineteenth century by scholars who thought it Greek. To its original audience it appeared a complex, classical allegory of that peerlessly classical subject, the elusiveness of reputation. *Pheme* runs away and the eager youth pursues, clutching his scroll; she thumbs her nose and sneers at him, "Nuts, pretty boy." What seemed classic once seems indelibly nineteenth-century now. *Pheme*'s gesture reveals her as a generically modern Fame; the young man's muttonchop whiskers mark him even more vividly as a nineteenth-century German scholar rather than one of his classic subjects (the scroll, it has brilliantly been suggested, must be his doctoral dissertation).[37] Similarly naive period features mar every forgery from Chatterton's, with its efforts to make fifteenth-century citizens of Bristol write antiquarian treatises in the manner of the eighteenth-century editions of the sixteenth-century scholar William Camden, to Nanni's, with its efforts to make ancient writers compile genealogical tables like the trees of consanguinity used by medieval lawyers.

The forger, in sum, treats his reader as a flight simulator treats a pilot; he offers a vivid image of the specific text and situation that he seeks to represent, but only a vague and obviously unreal one of their periphery. Like the pilot in training, the reader in question is mesmerized by the deliberately projected, scrupulously detailed image at the center of his gaze, and the illusion works. Once he steps back and contests it, its vague areas and false perspectives emerge with dramatic starkness and surprising ease. Simulation is not reality, after all—though its emotional and physical effects can be wrenching enough when its victim wears the proper blinders.

✴ 3 ✴

CRITICS: TRADITION
AND INNOVATION

THE GERMAN scholars of the late eighteenth and early nineteenth centuries were masters at creating and accepting elaborate hypotheses, some of which rested, like inverted pyramids delicately balanced, on a single point of evidence. Many of them found it easy to believe three impossible things, or more, before breakfast. Remarkably enough, however, they were even better at doubting than believing. They doubted the unity and perfection of works previously taken as models of neoclassical aesthetics, like Homer's *Iliad* and *Odyssey*, which Friedrich August Wolf and many successors dissected to reveal their underlying strata with sometimes excessive zeal. They doubted the accuracy and historicity of the elaborate narratives that had previously provided most educated men with their basic outline of ancient history, like Livy's *History of Rome*, the elaborate structure that Barthold Georg Niebuhr levelled in his effort to excavate the original oral traditions about Rome's early years. And they doubted the authenticity of a great many classical texts, from some of Cicero's speeches and letters to some of Homer's poems. Indeed, they elevated their desire and ability to doubt into a fundamental principle of scholarly method. They claimed that serious scholarship on any author or subject must begin with a critical survey and evaluation of the extant sources; this survey must determine, in an impartial and systematic way, the authorship of each relevant primary text. And no further excavation or construction could take place until the ground had thus been cleared for it.[1]

Ever since Wolf and his pupils formulated these principles explicitly in their monographs and lectures, the higher criticism, the form of criticism that identifies works as authentic or inauthentic, has seemed a modern German specialty, and even a German invention. To be sure, German scholars have done far more than anyone else to identify the classical, medieval, and early modern precedents for their form of higher criticism—to assemble, for example, the remnants of Alexandrian literary scholarship. The richest of all historical studies on forgery, Wolfgang Speyer's magnificent *Die literarische Fälschung im heidnischen und christlichen Altertum*, arranges material from virtually all primary and secondary sources on ancient criticism in a lucid, jargon-free, and mercifully concise account. Speyer reveals again and again the penetrating insight and meticulous attention to detail that Alexandrian and Christian scholars often brought to the tasks of higher criticism. Yet Speyer's book implies that the criticism now practiced differs fundamentally from that known before the last centuries. He suggests that criticism has become in modern times an objective study applied to all sources; criticism in antiquity was a subjective study applied to sources one wished to attack. The one forms part of philology, the other part of rhetoric; the one takes an impartial and exhaustive approach, the other a subjective and erratic one. This distinction is vitally important, as we will see, but it needs qualification and supplementation if it is to yield the fullest possible insight.[2]

If one goes back through the dark forests of early modern learning partially mapped in the great reference books of the eighteenth century—Bayle's *Historical and Critical Dictionary*, Brucker's *Historia critica philosophiae*, and Fabricius' *Bibliotheca Graeca*—one discovers that many of the apparently innovative and sophisticated nineteenth-century debates over the nature and authorship of forged and pseudepigraphical texts actually reenacted scripts already written in the Alexandrian Museum or the seventeenth-century University of Leiden. When nineteenth-century scholars examined the substance of the pseudo-Aristotelian treatise *De mundo*, a work dedicated to Alexander the Great, the reagents they applied to its content produced a variety of stains. These revealed Neoplatonic and Pythagorean as well as Aristotelian ideas in it. The tests they applied to its form revealed a non-Aristotelian language and general approach. The *Philologen* devised many ingenious theories to explain the intrusion of this work—perhaps by another writer of the same name, perhaps dedicated to another patron named Alexander—into the Aristotelian corpus. What they rarely said explicitly, and what many of them probably did not realize, was that both their analytical methods and their substantive conclusions had been anticipated for the most part two centuries and more before them, by Joseph Scaliger's favorite pupil, Daniel Heinsius, whose dissertation on the *De mundo* was a masterpiece of balanced philological reasoning.[3]

Many other classic texts as well, from Boethius' *Consolatio philosophiae* to the *Corpus Hermeticum*, have led similarly difficult afterlives, their reputations rising and falling in a repetitive curve as scholars' methods remained stable but their assumptions changed, and the play of critical energy on specific passages changed with them. If we follow the histories of single texts, then, we see no radical break around 1800, but a continual, modest movement, often following paths made long before.

In fact the great Germans of the generation of the 1790s were more modest than their own later historians and biographers. They saw themselves as practicing a traditional, not a novel, art, though admittedly they also thought they did so at a newly high level. They continually emphasized their debt to the higher critics who had gone before them. In particular, they stressed the importance of the scholars of the late seventeenth century, those avatars of the critical spirit of the Enlightenment and authors of *Critical Histories* of almost everything. Jean Mabillon, Bernard de Montfaucon, and Scipione Maffei reconstructed the history of scripts and devised crisp rules for determining the worth of Greek and Latin manuscripts, both documentary and literary. Jean Leclerc had provided *the* systematic statement of the principles of higher criticism, and offered dozens of examples to clarify them, in his *Ars critica*. Richard Simon had pointed to the many seams showing in those great composite texts, the Old and New Testaments. Jean Hardouin had used the evidence of ancient coins to argue the inauthenticity of virtually every ancient text except Pliny's *Natural History* and Horace's *Epistles* ("Virgil," he wrote, "never thought for a second of writing the

Aeneid"), and had thus given not just a monumental example of learned crankiness but a powerful impetus to critical scrutiny of all sources, the apparently genuine as well as the obviously suspect. Richard Bentley, finally, had demonstrated the inauthenticity of more than one supposed classic with unique learning and vigorous, simple arguments in his *Dissertation on the Epistles of Phalaris*, an essay consistently recommended to nineteenth-century students of classics as the preeminent classic of higher criticism, ancient or modern.[4]

If the great critics of the years around 1700 were held up as models of perennial value, however, even they were not represented as radical innovators. Bentley, Wolf told his students, "applied together, in a masterly way, all the arts that earlier scholars had applied in isolation to similar problems." This perception matched Bentley's own. His first significant philological essay, the *Epistola ad Millium* of 1691, emphasized that the supposedly classical verses quoted by ancient Jewish writers which criticized idolatry and preached monotheism could not be the genuine work of Sophocles. It ridiculed with equal zest the verses ascribed by the Greeks to the legendary poet Orpheus and the modern scholars who explained these using "the foolish trifles of the Cabalists." And it made merciless fun of those "men of elegant judgment who revere the oracles commonly ascribed to the Sibyl as the real effusions of that prophetic old lady, Noah's daughter."[5] All of these arguments, as Bentley knew, recapitulated those made a century before by Protestant scholars he admired, when Isaac Casaubon demolished the claims to antiquity of the *Hermetic Corpus* and Joseph Scaliger denounced both the Christians who "thought the word of God so feeble that they feared the kingdom of God could not be furthered without lies" and the pagans who filled lacunae in the lives of their great men, like Socrates, with forged letters and documents.[6]

The work of the generation of the 1680s and 1690s, in other words, is inconceivable without that of the generation of the 1580s and 1590s; and the members of that, in turn, looked still further back for their models. Scaliger, following the ancient philosopher Sextus Empiricus, saw the identification of spurious passages and whole works as the most profound and original task the critic had to perform: "this," he enthusiastically wrote, "penetrates into the most obscure sanctuaries of wisdom." And he saw the ancients as the great models in this highly technical realm of scholarship. "Only those Homeric verses which Aristarchus approved of were accepted; only those comedies of Terence which Calliopius approved of"; "the prince [of Latin critics] was Varro. His criticism taught that out of many plays, only twenty-one were by Plautus; they were later called 'Varronian.' "[7] No scholar of the late twentieth century could assert the mastery of the critic over his material, the scholar over the writer, more confidently than Scaliger did as he looked at the ancient history of his trade. Casaubon compiled information toward a systematic work on criticism in antiquity, which he did not live to complete; he too saw Alexandrian Homerists and Jewish Masoretes as the models for his own enterprise. We have already seen Cardano apply ancient critical methods as systematically as the ancient medical teachings that were his proper specialty.

The point here is not to attack Wolf's or Niebuhr's claims to innovation or to establish the rival ones of precursors; few pursuits are more trivial than the establishment of intellectual genealogies imbedded in no larger context and framed by no wider set of questions. Rather, it is to demonstrate that most early modern and a good many modern scholars believed that their work as critics derived from a long-standing intellectual and scholarly tradition. Any treatment of the history of criticism must plot its data on this axis of continuity or it will produce far too sharp a gradient of innovation when dealing with modern times. To avoid these distortions in measuring continuity and change in the history of criticism, we shall compare and contrast three exemplary critics, ancient, early modern, and modern, who dealt with some of the same texts and problems.

Porphyry (third century A.D.) is best remembered for his technical work in philosophy, and he was indeed proficient at various forms of that absorbing pursuit. A student of the Athenian rhetorician Longinus and of the greatest Neoplatonic system-builder of the time, Plotinus, whose biography he wrote, Porphyry arranged Plotinus' work into the systematic order of the *Enneads* and wrote an *Isagoge*, or introduction, to Aristotle's logic that would remain standard for more than a millennium in several languages and cultures. He also wrote treatises of his own on grammatical and philosophical subjects. His *Homeric Questions* dealt with the technical chestnuts of Homeric criticism that had provoked grammarians to debate with one another since the third century B.C.; his essay *The Cave of the Nymphs* was a classic exercise in allegorical exegesis of Homer, a systematic demonstration that the earliest and apparently crudest of Greek classics in fact contained a hidden and sophisticated message. He also wrote elaborately against the Christians and on behalf of the traditional religious beliefs and practices of the Greeks. To carry out this wide range of exacting tasks, Porphyry lived a real philosopher's life of unremitting intellectual work, occasional spiritual rapture, and asceticism; he married only late in life, and then out of a sense of duty (he was almost seventy years old, and his wife was a widow with seven children).[8]

Isaac Casaubon (1559–1614) lived a life of struggle and exhaustion rather than inspiration and asceticism. He married early and had many children, becoming the prototypical philoprogenitive scholar who writes enormous, learned books with his right hand while rocking the newest baby's cradle with his left foot. He never achieved a sage's detachment; his enormous diary records continual worry over low salaries, impermanent jobs, and the constant inability to work as hard as he wished (a characteristic entry begins "I rose at five—alas, how late!—and at once went to my study").[9] Nevertheless he produced scholarly works of a scale and number that would have more than done credit to his pagan forerunner. Like Porphyry he took a substantial interest in both literature and philosophy; he produced the long-standard Latin translation of Polybius' history of the rise of Rome and wrote brilliant, learned commentaries on Diogenes Laertius' *Lives of the Philosophers* and Athenaeus' *Deipnosophistae*. He also edited the works of Aristotle and Theophrastus.[10]

Richard Reitzenstein (1861–1931) resembles Casaubon more than Porphyry. A liberal Protestant who renounced theology for philology as a student, he too led a productive life as both professional scholar and family man. Trained by Johannes Vahlen in one of the most technical of classical disciplines, the history of ancient grammatical and lexical scholarship, he distinguished himself in his twenties as a creative solver of technical puzzles in the transmission and content of such superficially arid works as Festus' *De verborum significatu*. In his later years at the Universities of Strasburg and Göttingen, he turned his formidable technical abilities to the history of religion in the ancient world—pagan, Zoroastrian, Jewish, and Christian. Though he saw two sons die in World War I and tended to lose faith in his own theories over time, he was survived by a third son and celebrated for his learning by colleagues and pupils. He is remembered as one of the boldest of classical scholars in the most creative age of *Altertumswissenschaft*, the interdisciplinary German brand of classical scholarship. He combined the technical equipment needed to edit and comment on Greek magical and religious texts with the wide interdisciplinary interests characteristic of the Warburg Institute, with which he was closely associated.[11]

Porphyry took a deep interest in the literary questions that had long occupied critics, including forgery and plagiarism. One fragment from his works describes a formal banquet held in Athens in honor of Plato's birthday (which fell on the seventh of Thargelion, whenever that was). This was attended by Nicagoras the sophist, Apollonius the grammarian, Demetrius the geometer, and Calietes the Stoic, among others. It was, in short, a faculty dinner party; like most of its twentieth-century counterparts, it soon degenerated into learned gossip about the crimes of past and present scholars. One Maximus accused the historian Ephorus of stealing three thousand whole lines; Apollonius replied that Theopompus, whom Maximus respected, had plagiarized the orator Isocrates word for word. Nicagoras joined in, exposing Theopompus' plagiarisms from Xenophon. Apollonius began to expand the list of criminals, referring duly to important secondary works (like Latinus' *On the Books of Menander that Were Not by Him* and Philostratus' *On the Thefts of the Poet Sophocles*). And so it went.[12] Exposure of plagiarism and exposure of forgery, of course, go naturally together; both stem from the same sharp sense of literary property and individuality, and both require the same high level of attention to textual detail. Porphyry, in other words, not only had a good training in the grammarians' now traditional craft; he also lived among others who shared these painstakingly acquired skills and enjoyed exercising them.

But Porphyry went further than most other ancient literary detectives. He became, indeed, the leading authority of his time on forgery and pseudepigrapha—or at least on those that seemed to lend some measure of age and authority to intellectual and religious traditions he disliked. Though he respected Jesus, he attacked the Jewish and Christian revelations, pointing out many obvious errors and incongruities in the Old Testament and the Gospels. For example, he condemned the story of Jonah and the whale as ludicrous: "It is improbable and incredible that a man should have been swallowed up with his clothing on in the inside of a fish; or if this is meant figuratively, you ought to have the courtesy of explaining it."[13] He pointed out (wrongly) that a terrifying storm could not blow up on a small, calm body of water like the Sea of Galilee. And he argued, elegantly and presciently, that the frightening, precise prophecies of the Old Testament Book of Daniel, supposedly written during the exile in the sixth century B.C., were disguised history. If Daniel foretold the events of the second century B.C., when Hellenizers would profane the temple in Jerusalem, this proved only that he had written his book after the events it described.[14]

Porphyry honed his critical skills elaborately, reading widely in the scholarly literature of his time. When he showed, for example, that the Book of Daniel must be a forgery, he used Africanus' argument that the story of Susanna and the elders contained two puns "which seem to fit the Greek language rather than Hebrew." He went further than Africanus only when he drew the inference that the entire text, rather than the story of Susanna alone, "was an invention and not in circulation among the Hebrews, but a made-up story in Greek."[15] His combination of pagan and Christian learning made him a formidable specialist, one with whom no Christian scholar of his time could argue on equal terms. No wonder, then, that Christians responded not only by rebutting his arguments but also by beating him and burning his writings.[16]

Like Porphyry, Casaubon took an expert's interest in questions of authenticity. In his early commentary on Diogenes Laertius he pointed out that the poem *Hero and*

Leander, traditionally ascribed to the legendary poet Musaeus, Orpheus' near-contemporary, must really be the work of a "grammarian"—a Hellenistic learned poet.[17] In his copy of the mock-Homeric *Battle of the Frogs and Mice*, he noted perceptively that a poet who said, as the author of the *Battle* did, that he wrote on "tablets on [his] knee" could hardly have been blind, as Homer was.[18] And he dedicated a critical edition and commentary to the *Historia Augusta*, which he saw could not possibly be the work of the six separate authors to whom the manuscripts ascribed it. At least three of them, supposedly, had been born at the same time, had set out simultaneously to write the lives of the emperors, and had done their work "using styles so little divergent that it is as good as impossible to distinguish between them"—a set of coincidences which flies in the face of probability. His judgment has been fully confirmed, and extended to all the supposed authors, by modern research. Casaubon concluded that some single individual had put the texts together in their transmitted form, though he could not divine the motive that had led him to do so.[19]

Moreover, and perhaps more unusual, Casaubon was as adept at construction as at demolition. He rightly argued, in his edition of Theophrastus' *Characters*, that the text was genuine. True, the great critic Pier Vettori had pointed out that the text claimed to have been written by a man ninety-nine years old, while Theophrastus, according to his biographers, had died at eighty-five. But Casaubon thought it absurd to use one piece of external evidence to attack the authenticity of a book listed by the ancients among Theophrastus' works, written by an

Athenian of Theophrastus' time, and clearly appropriate to Theophrastus in style and subject matter alike. And he used the evidence of style and vocabulary, even more fully and precisely assembled, to prove that Gregory of Nyssa's *Third Letter* must be authentic even though it did not occur in the best manuscript, the *Codex Regius*.[20]

Like Porphyry, Casaubon whetted his sensitivity to fakes with every available means. He was the son-in-law of Henri Estienne, the greatest of all sixteenth-century Hellenists and the compiler of the *Thesaurus linguae Graecae*, the very work that Father Hase would help to update 250 years later. Estienne too knew a good deal about authenticity; it was from him that Casaubon learned that the Musaeus of the *Hero and Leander* was not the legendary bard of the Greeks. And it was in Estienne's edition—which included a note calling attention to non-Homeric features in the text's diction—that Casaubon did his critical reading of the *Frogs and Mice*.[21]

Reitzenstein, living in an age of greater specialization, dedicated himself even more intensively than his predecessors to pseudepigrapha and forgeries. His chosen field of study, the history of religious sentiment and behavior, was preeminently represented in the Greek world by sources claiming to be the work of divine beings or inspired prophets. His most impressive book, *Poimandres* (1904), was the first comprehensive effort to assemble all the evidence, manuscript and printed, direct and indirect, bearing on the Hermetic writings and their authors. Reitzenstein edited the texts critically, traced their history from the time of Jesus to his own day, and distilled from them a sharp, precise, and idiosyncratic history of the Hermetic community that produced them—a community, he claimed, founded between the second century B.C. and the second century A.D. by an Egyptian priest, who brought together in a single Gnostic system the Egyptian doctrine that the universe had been created by Ptah and the Eastern belief that man, while alive, was enslaved in matter but could free himself by pursuing a path of mystical illumination. Reitzenstein's specific reconstructions now seem highly arbitrary; they in fact did even in his own day, when he later decided that the Hermetic way of knowledge was indeed Eastern, but Iranian, not Egyptian, in origin—and transformed his history of Hermetic belief and practice accordingly.[22]

Reitzenstein pursued scholarly enlightenment in this area as eagerly as the Hermetic initiates had pursued spiritual enlightenment. He saw that texts and fragments of texts in a number of non-Western languages—Egyptian, Old Persian, Arabic, and others—offered information complementary to that in the Greek texts. A gregarious man who loved to read Greek texts with friends and students, he formed a series of loose alliances with Orientalists willing to initiate him into the mysteries of their traditions. In Göttingen, a world center of Oriental studies, he worked with the brilliant convert from Judaism, Mark Lidzbarski, and the Persian scholar F. C. Andreas, gaining access to rich collateral evidence, as he saw it, for his broad theories about the Eastern origins of all Greek thought, from Plato on—and especially of his beloved *Hermetic Corpus*.

Reitzenstein read pseudepigrapha with a skill and tact that are all too easily obscured by the now obvious flaws in his theories. He made clear, as few had before him, that forgeries needed subtle analysis rather than sarcastic dismissal even when the latter seemed most called for. For example, he pointed out that when the author of *Corpus Hermeticum* 16 claimed to offer a kind of religious revelation mere Greeks could not grasp, the claim, though conventional, was not meaningless. The author did want "to certify the source and to heighten the anticipation" for his reader, just as an ordinary forger would. But he also genuinely believed that the ordinary foreign unbeliever who picked up his book "would not understand it; indeed, for him it must remain dead, just because the vision [that it would inspire in an initiated reader] does not occur."[23] Without doing violence to the conventions of the genre, Reitzenstein deftly picked out the individual element in his text: the genuine religious feeling that sets the author of *Corpus* 16 apart from the author of Dictys the Cretan's Trojan War stories. This high level of sensitivity had rarely if ever been applied before to a forged text.

The three men were linked across the centuries by another, related set of concerns as well. All three employed their historical and critical skills—in strikingly different ways, to be sure—to establish the preeminent authority of the religious and philosophical doctrines they embraced. In each case the historical argument for authority was crucial. In the late-antique marketplace of ideas, as we have seen, an ancient or an oriental pedigree, or preferably both at once, was the most enticing guarantee a seer could give for the power and beauty of his revelation. In sixteenth-century Europe Catholics denounced Protestants for breaking with the historical tradition of Christianity, and Protestants like Casaubon replied that they wanted to restore the historical rites and values of early Christianity, which the Catholics had corrupted. In Germany around 1900 conservatives tried to prove the uniqueness of classical Greece and Christianity, and liberals, Jewish and Protestant alike, insisted on the organic connections between Semitic and Western races, Judaism and other Eastern religions, and the high achievements of Western culture.

Porphyry defended his Platonic sect against all purportedly older and more exotic rivals. At Plotinus' request, for example, he composed a refutation of a work attributed to Zoroaster, "which I showed to be entirely spurious and modern, made up by the sectarians to convey the impression that the doctrines they had chosen to hold in honour were those of the ancient Zoroaster."[24] Casaubon, similarly, defended the historical cause of Protestantism. His last great book was a concerted attack on the most elaborate of Catholic efforts to show the continuity between the early Church and that of the sixteenth century, the *Annales ecclesiastici* of Cesare Baronio.[25] Reitzenstein, finally, wrote his powerful synthetic work *Hellenistic Mystery-Religions* in order to show that the essential religious language of early Christianity, and above all that of Paul, was derived from the language already used by Hermetists and others to describe their religious experiences. He considered historical analysis of this kind vital, since only a sense of the true, multiple sources of Christianity could preserve Protestantism from the "creating of uniformity" and "the dominance of formulas." By reading Paul and Poimandres together, one would see that other cultures and religions had always lent their substance and forms of expression to the most creative brands of Christianity: "its inner strength has always consisted in the fluidity of its outer boundaries."[26] All three men practiced higher criticism, then, not only for the love of the subject but for what they saw as a higher ideological purpose.

Finally, all three men converged as critics on a single text; and this above all makes our comparison informative. The *Hermetic Corpus*, as we have already seen, was one of the richest of late-antique pseudepigrapha, a record of the religious experience and magical practices of small groups that tried to maintain the integrity of Egyptian culture long after they had lost political autonomy, religious uniformity, or even linguistic access to their own hieroglyphic sacred texts. Already in Porphyry's time coherent groups of these texts, similar but not identical to the *Corpus* as we now read it, were in circulation. Already they included passages that tried to present them as remote, oriental, and ancient. In both Porphyry's time and Casaubon's, most readers found the texts absorbingly profound and impressively ancient, a sober and satisfactory blend of Platonic philosophy and biblical theology. The church father Lactantius and the Neoplatonist Iamblichus both saw the revelations of Hermes as the genuine outpourings of an Egyptian demigod and prophet.[27] Marsilio Ficino delayed translating Plato into Latin, at the direct request of his patron Cosimo de' Medici, in order to translate Hermes first. Francesco Rolandello's blurb in the first printed edition of his work urged the reader, "whoever you are, grammarian or orator or philosopher or theologian," to buy Hermes "because for a small price I will enrich you with pleasure and profit."[28] Pietro Crinito, one of the most learned of early sixteenth-century scholars, found it easy to detect and denounce the modern forgeries of Nanni, but he saw the ancient forgeries of Hermes as unquestionable classics: devout, profound, and genuine. As late as the 1580s, Justus Lipsius, one of the greatest experts in Europe on the development of ancient philosophy, used the presence of "many mysteries and secrets of our law" in the writings of the Egyptian Hermes as direct and powerful evidence for the purity and utility of pagan philosophy.[29] Both Porphyry and Casaubon, then, cut against the grain of their cultures when they dissected Hermes. Reitzenstein, by contrast, cut with the grain; like many other scholars of his day, notably Aby Warburg, he had been inspired by the hermeneutical theories of Wilhelm Dilthey and the historical practices of Hermann Usener to use key terms in a liturgical or theological text as clues to the earlier traditions it must stem from. Yet he too encountered considerable opposition when he insisted on the debt of Christianity itself to dubious Eastern revelations.

Porphyry's attack does not survive in its original form. It must be reconstructed from the answers offered by Iamblichus, whose rebuttal is itself, curiously, a pseudepigraphical work attributed to a priest, one Abammon, which replies to Porphyry point by point. Iamblichus' exposition shows that Porphyry denied some of the basic principles—less historical than philosophical or literary—that underpinned the veneration of Hermes. He denied, for example, that "barbarous" words for incantation and foreign names of gods were in any sense more profound than Greek ones, an assumption that surely inspired all antique forgers' claims to be the translators of oriental originals. And he not only redated but attacked Hermes' philosophy of nature.

As usual in Porphyry, however, the historical arguments stand out as striking and original. Iamblichus writes that "the books which circulate under Hermes' name contain Hermetic opinions, even though they often use the language of the philosophers; for they were translated from Egyptian by men not unskilled in philosophy."[30] The implication is clear. Porphyry saw, as modern readers do, that the corpus of Hermetic texts known to him uses Greek philosophical terms; he asked, as he did about the story of Susanna, how these could possibly correspond to a base text supposedly couched in an alien language. Iamblichus could reply only that the translators must have been responsible. Here as in his attacks on the Bible and the spurious work of Zoroaster, Porphyry used history and philology to refute the claims of a supposedly ancient and oriental revelation.

Casaubon's attack, by contrast, is elaborately developed in more than one place and fully documented in the surviving sources. It began when he reread the *Hermetic Corpus* in preparation for his attack on Baronio, who had cited it credulously in the *Annales*. Point after point provoked Casaubon to formulate sarcastic, learned remarks, which he inscribed in the margins of his copy in his characteristic scrawl and developed at length in his final critique of Baronio. By the time Casaubon published his critique, he had scoured off the text's patina of authority at several points. He had pointed out refer-

ISAACI
CASAVBONI
DE REBVS SACRIS ET
ECCLESIASTICIS
EXERCITATIONES
XVI.

Ad Cardinalis BARONII
Prolegomena in Annales, & primam eorum
partem, de DOMINI NOSTRI
IESV CHRISTI Natiuitate, Vita,
Paßione, Assumtione.

AD
IACOBVM, Dei gratia, Magnæ
Britanniæ, Hiberniæ, &c.
Regem Sereniſimum.

LONDINI
Ex officina Nortoniana apud Ioan. Billium.
clɔ. Iɔ. C XIIII.
Cum privilegio Regis.

Plate 9. Controversy as the setting and motive for criticism. Isaac
Casaubon's attack on Hermes is a tiny part of this vast attack on
the Catholic church history of Cesare Baronio, dedicated to the
scholarly Protestant King James. I. Casaubon, *Exercitationes*
(London, 1614).

ences to Phidias and Eunomus, Greeks who lived long after the supposed age of Hermes. He had torn the text's supposedly antique diction to tiny shreds: "There are many words here," he wrote, "which do not belong to any Greek earlier than that of the time of Christ's birth."[31] These he listed in detail, using the occurrence of elaborate abstract nouns from the language of late pagan and Christian Neoplatonism and technical terms from Christian theology as irrefutable evidence of the lateness of the work. "Which of the older Greeks," he demanded, "would have used the word *authentia* for power? . . . Which of the earlier writers ever said *hulotes, ousiotes* and the like?"[32] Hermes had even made the particularly damning mistake of using the term *homoousios* (of the same substance), which showed that he must have had access to early Christian writings now lost.[33] Casaubon also detected clear borrowings from the Hebrew Bible on the one hand, in the Hermetic account of the Creation, and Plato's *Timaeus* on the other, in the Hermetic description of God as the perfect being who can feel no envy. And he had found evidence of a deliberate desire to deceive in the author's pretense to be offering a translation from the Egyptian. At one point the *Corpus* explains the etymology of the Greek term *kosmos: kosmei gar ta panta* (the universe is called *kosmos* because it imposes an order [*kosmei*] on everything). "Are . . . *kosmos* and *kosmei*," Casaubon demanded, "words from the ancient Egyptian language?"[34] Here, as in Porphyry's analysis of Daniel, the presence of a play on Greek words revealed the absence of an underlying original text in a Near Eastern language. The demonstration seemed irrefutable; even the Catholic polemicists who tried to refute Casau-

bon's views on virtually every other point on which he
attacked Baronio accepted his redating of the *Corpus*.[35]

If Casaubon's remarks are elaborate, Reitzenstein's
are baroque, both in their depth and in their protean reflection of Reitzenstein's own changing views of the subject. In *Poimandres*, in *Hellenistic Mystery-Religions*,
and in many longer and shorter essays, Reitzenstein analyzed the language, the form, and the content of the *Corpus* more systematically than had any of his predecessors. In his work the fact that the text was a forgery of
the imperial era served not as a conclusion but as a beginning. Once the text's pretensions were definitively set
aside and its real niche in chronology and geography was
established, its historical virginity was paradoxically re-
stored. It became a genuine document against its author's will, and so Reitzenstein used it. Its language became a key, rich in repeated formulas and glosses on its
own formulations, to that of more laconic and histori-
cally more important texts like the Epistles of Paul.
Where Paul referred to those who possess *gnosis* (knowledge) but lack *agape* (love), earlier exegetes had assumed
that *gnosis* meant "rational knowledge"; Reitzenstein
showed that it meant the way of supernatural knowledge
that Hermetists and Christian Gnostics thought could
lead them to a direct and transforming knowledge of
God. The *Hermetic Corpus* became not a shadow of the
New Testament but a torch to illuminate it; both Paul's
own views and those he attacked were transformed in
the light shed by this forgery, properly understood.[36]
Whatever the variations—and they were extreme—in
Reitzenstein's views about the ultimate origins of the
Hermetic doctrines, his use of the substance of the text

remains exemplary. No one has ever done more to breathe the life of religious feeling into the dry words of a document, or to call lost human dramas and rituals back to life from an austere and sketchy script.

This triple juxtaposition of Porphyry, Casaubon, and Reitzenstein is revealing in several ways. First of all, it shows that Casaubon's demonstration, often cited in modern times as a classic of higher criticism, did not use many arguments that were new in themselves. Porphyry had already seen that the diction of the *Corpus* was not reconcilable with its supposed great age and Egyptian identity. Casaubon could view the whole tradition of Greek literature from a strategic point outside it and had access to the vast range of editions of Greek texts and reference books on the Greek language produced in the sixteenth century. He made Porphyry's argument irrefutable by supplying the data it had left out. But in doing so he augmented the power of a general thesis that he did not invent.

In the second place, it shows that even if Casaubon asked a wider range of questions about the *Corpus* than Porphyry did, he did not radically alter or improve the methods of the higher criticism in doing so. In picking out anachronisms in the text, for example, Casaubon called attention to flaws that Porphyry did not, so far as we know, mention in this context. But the concept of factual anachronism was clearly familiar to Porphyry, who applied it deftly in his demonstration of the true age of the Book of Daniel. And in any event Casaubon did not discover the particular factual anachronisms that he criticized in the *Hermetic Corpus*. The fanatical Calvinist chronologer Matthaeus Beroaldus had already used them to attack the *Corpus* in his world chronology, and Casaubon—who owned Beroaldus' book and left a note at the passage in question in his copy, now in the British Library—clearly drew this point and its implications straight from his modern predecessor.[37]

In both of these respects, moreover, there is a clear difference in kind between Porphyry's or Casaubon's enterprise and that of Reitzenstein. The earlier critics were both, in a sense, doing only what came naturally: attacking a text that contained not only technical flaws that irritated their sensibilities but also heresies that offended their deepest convictions. Porphyry, the impassioned defender of the Greek religious tradition, found it easy to see through a text that maintained the preeminence of "barbarous" Egypt. Casaubon, even more explicitly, attacked the *Corpus* because it corresponded too closely to Plato and the Bible to be real. After all, he pointed out, to take the *Corpus* at face value meant assuming a separate and superior revelation to the Gentiles: "it seems contrary to God's word to think that such deep mysteries were revealed more clearly to Gentiles than to the people that God loved as peculiarly his own."[38] Neither Porphyry nor Casaubon could "prove" that barbarian culture was not older than Greek or that Egyptian theology was not basically Christian; they assumed these principles, which in turn both inspired and shaped their attacks on texts that violated them. Others who did not share the assumption might well deny its application, as did the seventeenth-century student of Persian religion, Thomas Hyde, when he admitted that his monotheistic interpretation of the religion of Zoroaster implied a separate revelation to Gentiles, and interpreted that in turn not as evidence of the impossibility of his views but as a sign of the unintelligibility of Providence.[39] In both cases, then, criticism meant using history to attack a text that was unacceptable for reasons that were not strictly historical. The contrast with Reitzenstein's willingness to accord full faith and credit, where appropriate, to a fake could hardly be sharper.

Our comparison does confirm the existence of a long tradition of critical thinking, one that was diversely applied but not fundamentally transformed over the centuries. It shows that both the classical and the early modern scholar used the same techniques we would when they set about studying a forgery: systematic juxtaposition of the language, substance, and stated and unstated assumptions of the document with those that other evidence would lead one to expect. But it also reveals that gradual but crucial changes took place between Porphyry's day and Casaubon's day. Casaubon felt freer than Porphyry did to cite his linguistic and other evidence in detail. Perhaps the rhetorical conventions of antiquity prevented Porphyry from achieving certainty at the cost of causing tedium; perhaps he felt that any educated reader should be able to spot the disfiguring neologisms in Hermes once his attention had been called to them in a general way. In any event, the chief distinction between Porphyry's argument and Casaubon's lies not in the sophistication of the methods employed but in the weight of the data amassed. And it is possible that weight of data is one vital distinction, more in general character than in technical method, between early modern and ancient higher criticism. Certainly it is one respect in which Casaubon and Reitzenstein stand together against Porphyry, who had no audience of professional scholars to appreciate a mass of detailed argument even if he had wished to provide one.

If the amount of evidence a Casaubon needed to manipulate was exponentially larger than the material his ancient counterpart had to use, the tools he could apply to it were also more varied. Casaubon, after all, could draw on two millennia of scholarly practice not only for specific remarks about Hermes but also for general methodological examples to imitate. And there is no doubt he did just that. In asserting that a pagan prophet could not have anticipated the truths of Christianity more fully and clearly than the Jewish ones did, Casaubon borrowed the argument that another Calvinist scholar, Johannes Opsopoeus of the Palatinate, had used a few years before to demolish another ancient forgery, the *Sibylline Oracles*. Opsopoeus had also used the clarity of his text, which he edited critically and surrounded with erudite commentary, as evidence that it must be fraudulent. It was too clear a prophecy to have been given by God to a prophet who did not belong to the chosen people: "Isaiah predicted vaguely: Behold a virgin will bear a boy. But the Sibyl does so by name: Behold a virgin named Mary will bear a boy Jesus in Bethlehem. As though the Prophets predicted the future with less divine inspiration than the Sibyls." And the text was in any event too lucid and elegant in its exposition of events to have been the result of an inspiration. The *Oracles* were really conscious compositions, the work "of a calm mind, not of divine madness [*animi sedati potius quam furoris*]."[40] Here Opsopoeus applied yet another classical tool to modern ends. Cicero, in *De divinatione*,

had argued forcefully that the acrostic *Sibylline Oracles*
he knew were too clear to be real prophecies, that they
must be the product "of a writer, not a raver [*scriptoris,
non furentis*]."[41] Opsopoeus' balanced phrasing reveals
his debt to Cicero beyond doubt. And the whole episode
exposes the vital difference between Casaubon's historical position—or Reitzenstein's, with its manifold further
multiplication of materials and techniques—and Porphyry's; it also confirms the intact presence of a large
antique component in Casaubon's most sharply modern
critical work.

Yet the coin has its other side. The three men shared
one vital characteristic perhaps more significant than
their differences: all showed far less critical discrimination when they dealt with texts that coincided with their
assumptions and desires. Porphyry saw through Hermes
easily enough. But when it came to the material about
early Phoenician history and religion assembled by Philo
of Byblos, his credulity proved as vast as his criticism
could be sharp. He accepted, and perhaps even ampli-
fied, Philo's claim to have drawn on the *Phoenician History* of Sanchuniathon of Beirut, who "as they say, lived
before the time of the Trojan War" and used "the treatises written by Hierombalos, the priest of the god
Ieuo."[42] And he did not, apparently, venture a word of
doubt about the genuine Phoenician origin of Sanchuniathon's work, even though it employed as one of its basic
methods the Hellenistic Greek assumption, often associated with the scholar Euhemerus, that the gods of ancient myth were in fact mortals considered divine by
later men because of their great deeds. The claim to have
used ancient Phoenician records now inaccessible, and

the application of the Alexandrian custom of bestowing honorary divinity on rulers of the primeval world of ancient myth, were exactly the sort of stereotypical forger's anachronisms that Porphyry could detect with ease when other, deeper prejudices impelled him to do so. And sometimes Porphyry moved even further from the critical standpoint with which he is normally and rightly associated. In his *Philosophy from Oracles* he collected oracles of the Greek gods in order to demonstrate that his own philosophical monotheism could be reconciled with the traditions of Greek religion and mythology. The enterprise sounds wholly laudable and straightforward until one encounters Porphyry, in his preface, explaining that he has "neither added anything, nor taken away from the sense of the oracles, except where I have corrected an erroneous phrase, or made a change for greater clarity, or completed the metre when defective, or struck out anything that did not fit the purpose"; one realizes that Porphyry was capable not only of accepting forgeries that fitted his needs and interests, but also of rewriting genuine texts when necessary.[43] Porphyry's philology could create spurious authorities as dextrously as it destroyed them.

Casaubon, similarly, could see the flaws in a Hellenized Egyptian's effort to show that his ancestors were already philosophical monotheists. But forgeries more sympathetic to his assumptions passed his critical examination unscathed. Though suspicious at first about the *Letter of Aristeas*, for example, he later decided that it really was genuine and pious—even though Scaliger, his friend and correspondent, easily picked out the chronological and other errors that disfigured it. After all, the letter made good learned Jews say suitably pious and philosophical things about the more repellent bits of the Old Testament; it was hard for any Calvinist of wide views and interests not to be captivated by story and dialogue alike.[44]

Reitzenstein too proved gullible when a text suited his need to find non-Western and non-Christian roots for Greek or Christian ideas. His whole theory of the Iranian origins of Greek thought—which resulted not only in a rewriting of his work on Hermes but in the production of what amounted to a novel about Plato and his student Eudoxus and their Persian learning—rested on one pseudepigraphical text, a Hippocratic medical treatise which he took to be early in date and Persian in content. But neither the age nor the foreignness of this treatise has seemed obvious to later scholars; while some would still consider Reitzenstein's view of the work tenable to some extent, no one would rear a whole edifice of cultural and religious history on so slender and shaky a foundation. And anyone can see that Reitzenstein did not subject this text to the rigorous search for sources and parallels that he made in the *Hermetic Corpus*.

The continuities seem almost as impressive as the changes in this long history. Whatever the changes in critics' assumptions, the basic set of tools the critics use today to pry open a forgery and see how and why it works would have been entirely familiar to Casaubon and probably to Porphyry as well. Their basic method is, quite simply, systematic comparison. Their conclusions are correct and irrefutable, so long as they rest on valid parallels (one strong parallel is infinitely better evidence, in all these cases, than any number of weak ones). And they go wrong, usually, for the very reasons that lead them into criticism in the first place: because they want to find evidence either to support a wider thesis which is philosophical or theological, not philological or historical, in character, or to support a philological or historical case which itself rests on unquestioned assumptions rather than testable evidence. In his own way Reitzenstein was as interested a reader and critic as Porphyry or Casaubon.

The arguments of the critics—ancient, modern, early modern—are organically related to one another. They belong to a coherent tradition that began in classical Greece. When Richard Bentley used anachronisms of language and content in the letters ascribed to Phalaris to show their inauthenticity, one of his many enemies made fun of what he treated as a novel and ludicrous procedure: "He knows the age of any Greek word, unless it be in the Greek Testament, and can tell you the time a man lived in by reading a page of his book, as easily as I could have told an oyster-woman's fortune when my hand was crossed with a piece of silver."[45] So the late astrologer William Lilly was made to ridicule Bentley in a dialogue of the dead written by William King. In fact, however, as we have seen, the historical use of language to date a document, and even to destroy its reputation, was not Bentley's invention but part of the classical tradition in scholarship. Higher criticism, in short, has been an object as well as the instrument of every effort to revive the classics.

** 4 **

FORGERY INTO CRITICISM:
TECHNIQUES
OF METAMORPHOSIS,
METAMORPHOSIS OF
TECHNIQUES

JOSEPH SCALIGER encountered two supernatural beings in the course of his long and well-spent life. He saw one of them, a black man on a horse, as he rode by a marsh with some friends. He only read about the other, a monster named Oannes with the body of a fish and the voice of a man. Yet as so often happened in the Renaissance, the encounter with Art had far more lasting consequences than that with Life. The black man tried to lure Scaliger into the marsh, failed, and disappeared, leaving him confirmed in his contempt for the devil and all his works: "My father didn't fear the devil, neither do I. I'm worse than the devil."[1] Oannes, in the book that Scaliger read, climbed out of the ocean and taught humanity the arts and sciences. Devil Tempts Man, in the Renaissance, was no headline to excite the public; Amphibian Creates Culture was something very far out of the ordinary.

The fish who gave us civilization appeared at the beginning of the account of Babylonian mythology and history written by Berosus, priest of Bel, early in the third century B.C. Berosus drew on genuine Babylonian records but wrote in Greek, for the benefit of the Seleucid king Antiochus I Soter. Like so many other Near Eastern writers of the time, he tried to avenge in the realm of the archive a defeat on the battlefield, using documents and inscriptions to show that Babylon was older and wiser than Greece. Unlike some of the others, he offered a genuine account of traditional beliefs about the gods and the past. Jewish and Christian writers preserved his *Babyloniaca*.[2] It was in the unpublished world chronicle of one of them, George Syncellus (ca. A.D. 800), that Scaliger met Berosus and his fishy pet, in 1602 or 1603.

The most remarkable thing about the encounter was Scaliger's reaction to it. As a good Calvinist he considered ancient Near Eastern gods to be abhorrent and Hellenistic Near Easterners' boasts of the great antiquity of their civilization to be fanciful. As a good scholar, moreover, Scaliger knew that Berosus was not a name to inspire much trust. Throughout his career as a historian and chronologer, which began with the publication of his great treatise *De emendatione temporum* (*On the Correction of Chronology*) in 1583, Scaliger had been one of the sharpest critics of Nanni's forged texts, which included, as a central component, a world chronicle attributed to Berosus. Scaliger complained bitterly that "everyone still follows [Nanni] in chronology," and strewed his technical treatises with nasty remarks about the Dominican's "deliramenta."[3] Yet in this case he showed respectful interest in what he had every reason to dismiss as mad forgeries. Taking his first notes on the story of Oannes, he remarked only that in another account the same being was called Oes, and added a remark about Berosus himself from the early Christian writer Tatian.[4] Compiling his last large work on world history, the *Thesaurus temporum* of 1606, Scaliger included all the Berosus he could find, dated the material as precisely as he could, and boasted of the service he had performed by collecting these previously unknown texts.[5] He did not even remark, as Casaubon mildly did, when taking his own notes on the same manuscript chronicle, that "the nature of a certain animal, *Oannes,* is particularly curious [*in primis mira*]."[6] Instead, Scaliger defended the work of Berosus—like that of Manetho, which he also recovered and published—as genuine Near Eastern historiography, the early sections of which were indeed "fabulous," but which should be preserved both for the sake of the proper "reverence for antiquity" that Livy had shown for the traditions about early Roman history and because "the true records of the intervening period are directly connected with" them.[7] He thus offered the modern world its first genuine large-scale products of the ancient Near East, works so alien to the Western tradition that they could hardly be interpreted at all until the discovery and decipherment of parallel records in cuneiform, more than two hundred years later.

Scaliger's divinatory prowess—his ability to shake off the prejudices normal to his period and place and see that his Near Eastern fragments, if unintelligible, were also unimpeachable—seems to mark a dramatic new stage in the development of the higher criticism. And the tendency of historians has been to treat it as exactly that: the culmination of developments that took place throughout the fifteenth and sixteenth centuries, eventually giving rise to a newly effective critical method. Like the Hellenistic period and the early nineteenth century, in short, the Renaissance has been represented as the scene of a revolution in scholarship. The humanists of the early Renaissance tested and rejected many forgeries. The theologians and jurists of the mid-sixteenth century, men like Melchior Cano and Jean Bodin, were confronted by a much wider range of supposedly authoritative texts and an even more pressing set of religious and political problems. Accordingly they devised more thoroughgoing solutions. They had not only to purify the canon of its fakes but to weigh the authority of its genuine components. Accepting the humanists' isolated but valid insights, Cano and Bodin tried to fuse them into an art of choosing and reading authorities about the past. They provided not empirical case studies but universally applicable rules for evaluating sources, rules which reached a wide public in Bodin's powerful, popular, and polemical work on the *Method for Acquiring Knowledge of History with Ease* (1566).[8] It was presumably by applying these consistently to a wide range of texts that such slightly later scholars as Estienne, Scaliger, and Casaubon purged the classical corpus of its fakes and pseudepigrapha. The image conjured up is of a train in which Greeks and Latins, spurious and genuine authorities sit side by side until they reach a stop marked "Renaissance." Then grim-faced humanists climb aboard, check tickets, and expel fakes in hordes through doors and windows alike. Their revised destination, of course, is Oblivion—the wrecking-yard to which History and Humanism consign all fakes. Only humanists and genuine classics will remain on board to wind up as part of the canon. This vision suggests that the critical method of the humanists was both new and modern. Two centuries and more after the Renaissance, when Karl Otfried Müller confronted the Greek account of Phoenician antiquities forged by a young man named Wagenfeld, attributed to a mysterious disappearing manuscript from Portugal (and accepted by the Orientalist Grotefend), he needed only to apply the humanists' touchstones to make the appearance of authenticity vanish. Pseudo-Philo of Byblos, as presented by Wagenfeld, misunderstood and contradicted the fragments of his own work preserved by Eusebius (though he faithfully retained typographical errors from Orelli's printed text of the *Praeparatio Evangelica*). He made many unlikely grammatical and syntactical errors, large and small ("Auch im Gebrauche der Partikeln ist manche Unrichtigkeit zu bemerken"— "We can also note many errors in the use of particles"). And he believed in the gods (though he had really been an atheist). Müller transcended the humanists only in his sympathy for forgery as an art. He praised Wagenfeld's *Geist* and *Phantasie,* especially the splendid aptness with which he had caught "the spirit of ancient, Greek-Oriental historiography."[9] In other respects, however, he was merely doing what came humanistically.

Recent work on forgery, however, has added some attractive bends to this distressingly rectilinear account. Werner Goez has argued that previous historians omitted not just an important junction, but the crucial one, from their account of the ride of the ancients. Nanni, he points out, created not only texts but general and plausible rules for the choice of texts as well. These rules in turn formed the basis of all later systematic reflection on the choice and evaluation of sources. Some of the mid-sixteenth-century theorists, like Melchior Cano, rejected Nanni and all his works; others, like Jean Bodin, accepted them. But all of them developed their theories of reading in direct response to the challenge he presented. Thus, a forger emerges as the first really modern theorist of critical reading of historians—a paradox that only a reader with a heart of stone could reject.[10] More recent studies by Walter Stephens and Christopher Ligota have deepened our appreciation for Nanni's sensitivity to methodological issues in the choice of texts, and for the many fruitful hints he dropped in the course of justifying the use of his fakes.[11] Scaliger could tell that his Berosus was real; but did he owe his perceptiveness in large part to the creator of the false Berosus he despised?

Nanni wanted not to complement but to replace the Greek historians. As a good Dominican he knew that convincing arguments had to rest on unchallengeable general principles. Accordingly he insinuated, into both his forged texts and his commentaries, explicit, coherent rules for the choice of reliable sources. Metasthenes, one of his "authors," states these clearly:

> Those who write on chronology must not do so on the basis of hearsay and opinion. For if they write by opinion, like the Greeks, they will deceive themselves and others and waste their lives in error. But error will be avoided if we follow only the annals of

the two kingdoms and reject the rest as fabulous. For these contain the dates, kings, and names, set out as clearly and truly as their kings ruled splendidly. But we must not accept everyone who writes about these kings, but only the priests of the kingdom, whose annals have public and incontrovertible authority, like Berosus. For that Chaldean set out the entire Assyrian history on the basis of the ancients' annals, and we Persians now follow him alone, or above all.[12]

Nanni's comment expanded on Metasthenes. He described the ancient priests as "publici notarii rerum gestarum et temporum," "public recorders of events and dates," whose records deserved as ready belief as the notarial records in a modern archive. And his other authors repeated and expanded on these injunctions. After working his way through Myrsilus, Berosus, and Philo, the reader knew that each of the Four Monarchies (Assyrian, Persian, Greek, and Roman) had had its own priestly caste and produced its own sacred annals.[13] Only histories based on these deserved credit, and any given historian deserved credit only for those sections where he drew on an authoritative set of records. For example, Ctesias the Greek "is accepted for Persian history and rejected from Assyrian history," since he drew his account of the former from the Persian archives (in fact, of course, he invented it) and made the latter up.[14] Ordinary Greek historians deserved only contempt.

These principles do seem the result of a prescient effort to separate history, the record of events (*res gestae*) from history, the literary work of an individual (*histo-*

ria). And they certainly mark an effort to replace the empirical, case-by-case practices of the early humanists with a general theory. But as Stephens has shown in absorbing detail, they were as traditional in substance as they seemed to be novel in form.[15] In the last years of his life, the Jewish historian and honest traitor Josephus wrote a polemical work in two books against the grammarian Apion, who had defamed the Jews. In the course of this, Josephus, like his Hellenistic predecessors, repeatedly emphasized the novelty of Greek and the antiquity of Jewish civilization. And to drive this point home he emphasized that the Jewish and Near Eastern texts he quoted rested not on individual opinion but on archival documents recorded by a caste of priests:

> The Egyptians, the Chaldeans, and the Phoenicians (to say nothing for the moment of ourselves) have by their own account an historical record rooted in tradition of extreme antiquity and stability. For all these peoples live in places where the climate causes little decay, and they take care not to let any of their historical experiences pass out of their memory. On the contrary, they religiously preserve it in their public records, written by their most able scholars. In the Greek world, however, the memory of past events has been blotted out.[16]

Josephus elsewhere praises Berosus for "following the most ancient records," the people of Tyre for keeping careful "public records," and the Egyptians for entrusting the care of their records to their priests.[17] And if the *Contra Apionem,* available in Latin since the time of Cassiodorus, was little read in the Middle Ages, Nanni certainly used it heavily, in one of the fifteenth-century editions that gave it a vast new currency. In fact, in his comment on Metasthenes Nanni made clear in his usual way what his source was. He explains that "Josephus used Metasthenes' rules to make a most valid argument" against Greek views on the origin of the Greek alphabet.[18]

Nanni's rules, then, were not his own creation. In content they were a classical revival, for the most part a restatement of that partly justified Near Eastern pride in great longevity and accurate records that animated so much of the resistance to Hellenization and to Rome, and gave rise in its own right to so many forgeries. In form they transplanted the legal and notarial practices of Nanni's day, with their emphasis on the proper form and public attestation of documents, back into his imagined ancient world. We will not find in Nanni's rules alone the origins of modern historical hermeneutics.

What then of the methodologists who followed Nanni, those intellectuals of very different origins and types, from the Spanish Dominican Melchior Cano to the irenic lawyer François Baudouin, who confronted the same set of theoretical and practical problems two generations later, and whose works were the familiar, fashionable reading of Scaliger's youth? All had to find guidance for churches split on points of dogma, kingdoms split along multiple social and religious fault lines, and families divided by both religious and political questions. And all agreed that the authoritative canon of ancient texts, biblical and classical, should provide the remedies needed to heal the fissures in church and state and quell the European trend toward religious and civil war. Read-

ing was urgent, but reading unguided by rules led only to
chaos, as the Reformation clearly showed. Accordingly,
the mid-century saw a massive effort to rethink and reg-
ulate the reading of the ancients—particularly the historians, those preeminent guides for practical action in the
present. Which sources were which? This simple question burned for two decades. Could it be that these later
texts, rather than Nanni's *Antiquitates*, were the context
in which rules of a distinctly modern critical method
crystallized?[19]

In fact, as we will see, the new rules had a great deal to
do with Nanni's old ones. The false Berosus and his
brethren had a lively and productive afterlife in the sixteenth century, and the critical ideas Nanni laid out in
them long remained relevant and attractive. We can begin with Postel, a strange man, half visionary and half
philologist, who started out in religious life in the early
Jesuit order and wound up honorably confined as a
learned, harmless madman in a French convent. A real
scholar, one who knew Greek well enough to compile a
pioneering study of Athenian institutions and who had a
full command of Hebrew and other Eastern languages,
Postel cherished prejudices even more overpowering
than his erudition. He saw classical Greek and Roman
culture as a perversion of an earlier, Near Eastern revelation, best entrusted in his own day to the virtuous Gauls;
he condemned Romulus as a descendant of Ham who
had tried to extirpate the virtuous laws and customs
established in Italy by Noah, also known as Janus.[20]
He knew that some doubted the authenticity of Berosus
and the rest, but he stoutly maintained the positive,
accepting the texts and Metasthenic rules as givens:

"Though Berosus the Chaldean is preserved in fragments, and is disliked by Atheists or enemies of Moses,
he is approved of by innumerable men and authors expert in every language and field of learning. Hence I
grant him the faith deserved by any accurate author."[21]
At the other end of the spectrum we find Baudouin, writing in 1560, expressing his surprise that so many of his
contemporaries had accepted as genuine the "farrago"
of Berosus, with its many obvious falsehoods.[22] On the
one hand unquestioning faith and reverence, on the
other the disgust of a gardener confronted by a poison-
ous spider; as one would expect, neither position rests on
elaborate argument.

Between the extremes, the positions grow more complex and the supporting arguments, or at least the supporting attitudes, more subtle. On the side of credulity
we find John Caius of Cambridge, a skilled Hellenist, like
many sixteenth-century medical writers, and one with a
sharp interest in questions about lost and inauthentic
medical works from the ancient world. In the 1560s he
became embroiled in a dispute with Thomas Caius of
Oxford about the age of their two universities. Trying to
prove the antiquity of learning in England, he cited Berosus copiously about the giants Sarron and Druys, who
founded public institutions of learning in England and
Gaul around the year 1829 after the Creation, a bit more
than 150 years after the Flood. Yet for all his apparent
belief in the learned Sarronidae and Berosus "antiquae
memoriae scriptor," he took care to indicate that the
giants had not founded Cambridge—that came later—
and, more important, that the giants had been so called
not because they were huge but because they were abo-

rigines (*gegeneis*). True, one or two of them, like Pol-
yphemus and Gogmagog, had reached great heights, but
on the whole "giants, like modern men, came in a variety
of sizes," even if nature brought forth stronger and big-
ger offspring in those purer days. By confining his use of
Berosus to this very early period, by rationalizing away
some of his more bizarre ideas, and by faith, Caius could
avoid applying to the myths that supported his own position the cutting-edge, philogical criticism he applied to
classical medical texts and Oxford myths about the academic beneficence of Good King Alfred.[23] And a similar
attitude—of distrust mingled with unwillingness to give
up such rich material—can be found in others, like the
historian Sleidanus, the historical theorist Chytraeus,
and, perhaps, Caius' younger Oxford contemporary
Henry Savile.[24]

On the side of criticism we find a number of writers—
the theologian Cano, the Portugese scholar Gasper Barreiros, the Florentine antiquary Vincenzo Borghini—pil-
ing up evidence to prove the falsity of the Annian texts.
They rapidly found in his richest ancient sources ample
evidence of his mistakes. Berosus, in Josephus, explicitly
denied the Greek story that Semiramis had converted
Babylon from a small town to a great city; the Berosus in
Nanni's corpus affirmed it. Josephus' Berosus wrote
three books, Nanni's wrote five.[25] And in any event Josephus' Berosus knew only about events before his own
time, while Nanni's mentioned the founding of Lug-
dunum, which took place two hundred years after his
death.[26] These critics, moreover, did not confine themselves to pointing out blunders of organization and detail. They also showed that Berosus wrote the wrong

kind of history for his age and place. The Greeks of his time, after all, knew nothing about western lands like Spain; how could Berosus, still farther east than they, know more?[27] And as to the "annals" of the Greeks and Romans, Cano pointed out in a brilliant historiographical essay that none existed. Josephus, Nanni's main source, denied that the Greeks had had designated public historians. And Livy, the main source for early Roman history, showed by his infrequent citation of public records and his many errors and hesitations that "there were no public annals in the libraries and temples of the gods." Cano's conclusion was remorseless: "Those who say that the Greek and Roman monarchies had public annals against which other histories must be checked say nothing. . . . For it has been shown that no Greek or Roman public annals existed. Therefore there were no authors who described deeds or times in accordance with those Greek and Roman annals."[28] Here the limits of Nanni's own historical imagination told against him. A more modern notion of the practice of classical historians revealed that they were rarely if ever "public recorders of events."

Still more complex were the reactions of the Wittenberg chronologer Johann Funck. A student of Philipp Melanchthon and a friend of Andreas Osiander, who wrote the celebrated and misleading preface to Copernicus' *De revolutionibus*, Funck attacked the records of the ancient world with both philological and scientific tools. These soon enabled him to chip away the authority of one of the deadliest Annian writers, Metasthenes, who covered the centuries just before and after the Babylonian exile of the Jews, for which neither the Bible nor any pagan author offered a full, coherent, and acceptable narrative. Like Copernicus and some earlier Byzantine writers, Funck set out to use the data preserved by Ptolemy, the great ancient astronomer. Like them, he wrongly identified Salmanassar, a king of Assyria mentioned in the Bible, with Nabonassar, the king of Babylon from whose accession on 26 February 747 B.C. the Babylonian astronomical records used by Ptolemy began. Unlike them, he systematically teased out the implications of astronomy for history. He identified the biblical Nabuchodonosor (incorrectly by modern standards) with the king Nabopolassar mentioned by Ptolemy. He pointed out that Ptolemy fixed the beginning of Nabopolassar's reign absolutely, since he dated a lunar eclipse to "the fifth year of Nabopolassar, which is the 127th year from Nabonassar [21–22 April 621 B.C.]."[29] He found a different epoch date for Nabuchodonosor in Metasthenes. And he concluded that Metasthenes, or the archives he had used, must be rejected: "Do not let his authority stand in your way. Rather examine how far he stands in agreement with Holy Scripture and Ptolemy's absolutely certain observations of times. That way, even if you do not manage to reach the absolute truth you may approach it as closely as is possible."[30]

Having examined a full range of texts, Funck also decided that ancient historians could lead when astronomical records gave out, so long as they were critically chosen: Herodotus and Eusebius, not Ctesias and Metasthenes, should be preferred.[31] He thus pioneered the way along what remains the only path to exact dates in ancient history. Though he, like the reader he addresses, did not reach the truth, his footing was remarkably sure.

Yet Funck found no stimulus in his examination of Metasthenes to raise wider questions about Nanni's writers or their archives. Where the early pages of Luther's world chronicle offered chaste white spaces, Funck's swarm with the deeds of the giants and the first seven Homers, all derived from Annian sources. Funck considered Berosus "the most approved history of the Babylonians" and copied him out joyfully, invention by invention.[32] Thus technical methods of a strikingly modern kind could coexist with a credulity so complete as to be surprising.

Bodin struggled mightily with Nanni's texts and Funck's ideas. He knew enough to add guarded references to the possible falsity of Berosus' and Manetho's fragments in his bibliography of historians, but not enough to do the same for Metasthenes or pseudo-Philo (or, indeed, for Dictys and Dares).[33] He quoted Metasthenes' advice about choosing historians without a word of caution, and praised Metasthenes as a historian who used archival sources and wrote about a people not his own (about which he could be objective).[34] And when it came to the problems Funck raised, he showed a shattering lack of perceptiveness. Berosus and Metasthenes disagreed with "the rule of celestial motions" not because they made mistakes or used bad sources, Bodin argued, but because they had not recorded the years and months of interregna. If only they had done so, like that "scriptor diligens" Ctesias, all discrepancies would drop away and all good sources hang together in one happy historical family.[35] Bodin's willingness to accept pagan attacks on Christianity as the product of milieu and education rather than moral debility marks him cleuo vfque ad annum Chrifti M. D. LII.

Status ecclefiæ incerti autoris, à Chrifto nato vfque ad annum M. D. L X.

Clar.1548.   Io. Sleidani hiftoria ecclefiaftica, ab anno Chrifti M. D. X V I I. vfque ad annum M. D. L V. Hiftoriæ Magdeburgicæ centuriæ duodecim à nato Chrifto vfque ad annû M. C C. quibus veterum omnium fcripta ecclefiafticæ hiftoriæ copiosè explicantur.

De ftatu religionis & ecclefiæ fub regibus Henrico 11. Francifco 11. & Carolo 1 x. incerti autoris. Gal.

Hiftorici fectæ Arabicæ.

Clar.anno   Coranus feu Furcanus, ex omnibus Cora-
Chr.600.   nis, qui Muhamedis nomine circunferebantur, collectus anno poft Muhamedem c x.

Hiftorici Caldæorum, Aßyriorum, Medorum, Ægyptiorum, Perfarum, Phœnicum, Hebræorum, Parthorum: quorum geſta funt ab iifdem ferè fcriptoribus comprehenfa.

Libri Regum, Paralipomenæ & Efdræ.
Clar.ante   Herodoti Halicarnaffæi libri nouem hifto-
Chr.445.   riarum.

Ctefię

Ctefiæ Cnidij, Agatharchidis & Mennonis fragmenta, de regibus Perfarum & Afsyriorum.   Clar. anno Chr.375.

Xenophontis Athenienfis, de expeditione Cyri (cuius fuit legatus) in Perfidem.   Clar. ante Chr.370.

Berofi facerdotis Caldæi fragmenta, quæ feruntur, libris quinque comprehenfa.   Clar. ante Chr.340.

Metaſthenis Perfæ, de iudicio temporum & annalium Perfarum liber.   Clar. ante Chr.130.

Manethonis facerdotis Ægyptij fragmenta, quæ feruntur, de Regibus omnium penè populorum.   Clar. ante Chr.330.

Iofippi libri duo aduerfus Appioné Grammaticum, ac x x. antiquitatum Iudaicarum.   Clar. anno Chr. 99. Clar.130.

Hegefippi liber 1. de bello Parthico.   Clar.140.
Appiani Parthicus.
Procopij de bello Perfico libri 11.   Clar.540.

Hiftorici Græcorum, quo nomine veniunt Iones, Æoles, Dores, qui Afiam minorem & Europam, à Danubio, Actocerauniis, & Hemo monte, vfque ad mare Ionicum, in infulis & continente, fedes fixerunt.

Dictys Cretenfis de bello Troiano, libri v 1. è lingua Punica in Latinam à Q. Septimo conuerfi.   Clar. ante Chr.1129.

P 2   Da-

Plate 10. The difficulties of a pioneer. Jean Bodin provided the first bibliography of historians in his *Methodus ad facilem historiarum cognitionem*. Note that it contains both ancient fakes and Renaissance ones by Nanni, whose work he strip-mined for both facts and ideas. Thus the forger's work was deeply embedded in that of the historical critic. From J. Bodin, *Methodus* (Paris, 1572).

as an unusually perceptive reader. But his use of Metasthenes sets narrow limits on his critical faculties and reveals that Nanni helped to inspire, and even to shape, his notion of critical method. And even Bodin's insistence that the accuracy of historians be judged case by case, not in a single verdict—his belief that Dionysius of Halicarnassus, for example, described Roman foreigners more objectively than he described his fellow Greeks, and therefore should be read in different ways at different points—even this is no more than a development of Nanni's argument that a single historian could be accepted as a source with regard to one kingdom and still rejected as unreliable for another. Bodin's rich tapestry of methodological admonitions reveals many gaudy Annian splotches when held up to the light. And his weaknesses as a historical critic are all the more striking when compared to the great strengths of the forgotten Johann Funck, whose work he knew so well.

The most complex and one of the most influential of all the mid-century readers was Joannes Goropius Becanus, the Flemish doctor whose *Origines Antwerpianae* of 1569 mounted the shrewdest attack of all on Nanni, and in doing so drew on much of the literature we have surveyed. To refute the forgeries he collected as many fragments as possible, in Greek, of the real authors Nanni had travestied. Again and again he showed by direct inspection of original evidence (which Nanni, knowing only Latin, had had to use at second hand) that Nanni's fakes were not only derivative but grossly inaccurate. Nanni, for example, following a passage in Saint Jerome's Latin translation of the world chronicle by Eusebius, wrote a text in which the poet Archilochus expressed an opinion about the date of Homer's life. Goropius knew that Archilochus was a poet, not a scholar. Goropius also knew Greek, and in the vast collection of information assembled by the church father Clement of Alexandria, the *Stromateis*, he found the Greek original of the statement Nanni had followed. This, however, turned out to be a statement about Archilochus, not one by him; it was attributed to a real historian, Theopompus, who had suggested that Homer and Archilochus were contemporaries. Goropius thus revealed both that Nanni's Archilochus was a fake and that it was derived from a late and corrupt Latin version of an original Greek source.[36] In short, he found inspiration in Nanni not to advance theories but to collect fragments and elucidate them, and by doing the latter he made the first systematic progress toward reconstructing the history of critical historiography in the ancient world. The *Origines Antwerpianae* are the distant ancestor of *Die Fragmente der griechischen Historiker*, the vast edition of fragments of the Greek historians by Felix Jacoby which has revolutionized this field in the twentieth century.

Yet Goropius had more in mind than negative criticism and technical philology. He had his own new history of the ancient world to advance, one in which the Dutch were the remnant of the antediluvian peoples and their language, with its many monosyllables, was the primal speech of Adam. To prove this he offered evidence of many kinds, notably the famous experiment of king Psammetichus, who locked up two children, did not let them learn to speak, and found that they spontaneously asked for "Becos," the Phrygian word for bread, thereby identifying the Phrygians rather than the Egyptians as the primeval race. This showed, Goropius reasonably argued, that the Dutch were the oldest; after all, "they call the man who makes bread a *Becker*. That king's ancient experiment shows that the language of the inhabitants of Antwerp must be considered the oldest, and therefore the noblest."[37] This revision of world history—which, as even Goropius admitted, rested on novel readings of the sources—was closely related to Goropius' attack on Nanni. An essential element of his history of the migrations lay in a denial of Nanni's thesis that Noah and his fellows had been giants; thus prejudice as well as precision inspired Goropius' sedulous work as collector and exegete.

The mid-century, then, saw a concerted effort to reshape the history of the world and to rethink the sources from which it should be derived. But the now-famous historical theorists like Bodin contributed less to this effort than did Gradgrind chronologers like Funck and wild fantasts like Goropius. No single writer, no single genre held a monopoly on the relevant forms of criticism; fantasists on some points were the grimmest and most exacting of realists on others. Twenty years of ardent speculation, most of it provoked by Nanni, left his forged texts and his tarted-up ancient critical rules firmly in command of large parts of the historical field as most scholars viewed it. But at least one of his attackers, Goropius, had already seen the path to accurate knowledge that Scaliger would take after 1600. Had Nanni not produced and distributed his fake fragments so effectively, research into the real ones might not have begun, and they would certainly not have been so intensively pursued.

Goez, then, is triumphantly right to point to the pervasive stimulus Nanni afforded, but wrong to overemphasize his isolation and originality. And the efforts of other scholars to locate in the methodological speculations of the sixteenth century the rise of a new and effective method of source criticism are surely wrong. The sixteenth-century theorists speculated cogently and originally about the mechanics and psychology of historical writing. But to describe their views as modern is to ignore their specific dependence on Nanni and their general inability to discriminate between genuine and forged sources. And to do that is to commit what has been described as a "hagiographical anachronism"—to attribute to the original and learned thinkers of the past ideas and methods consistent not with their assumptions and abilities but with ours.[38] The mid-sixteenth-century scholars engaged in source criticism of highly varied kinds, some conducted by rules that we would still accept but some by rules that we find it hard even to restate. The most original technical work of all, that of Goropius, was far more original in execution than in conception.

Meanwhile, back in Leiden, how did Scaliger manage not to reject the real Berosus as he had the false one? None of the writers we have examined could have taught him to accept as somehow generally reliable a text much of whose factual content was false. Whence came enlightenment?

In the first place, Scaliger's inspiration came from the same source as Goropius' did—from the stimulus afforded by Nanni to dig in the great Greek compilations by Josephus, Eusebius, Clement, and others for real fragments to set in place of the Annian ones. The longer Scaliger worked at history and chronology, the more urgent the collection of genuine sources and the expunging of forged ones seemed to him. In the second edition of his *De emendatione temporum* in 1598, Scaliger inserted a long appendix of Greek fragments from historical texts, and extensive comments of his own. Here he discussed Porphyry and Sanchuniathon; here he printed and explicated fragments of the real Berosus, drawn from Josephus and Eusebius. As for the *Thesaurus temporum* of 1606, much of it was given over to a vast anthology of fragments and whole texts bearing on ancient history, including such still vital documents as Manetho's lists of Egyptian dynasties and Ptolemy's *Canon* of the rulers of Babylon—which Scaliger first, in his notes, rejected as an impudent forgery and then saw to be genuine and consistent with other historical and astronomical records. In the same period of his life, Scaliger extended his inquiries into a wide range of other questionable texts as well. As a young man, he had marvelled at the *Hermetic Corpus*, which he described as "even more exciting [than Philo Judaeus] and very old indeed." As an old man, he demolished Dictys, Dares, Aristeas, and the *Sibylline Oracles* with equal zest, and found an ally of equal critical zeal and learning in Casaubon.[39]

Yet in one sense Scaliger went even further than Casaubon did; he saw that Manetho and Berosus were not only real Hellenistic Greek texts but real, if pale, representations of far older sets of records from the Near East. The texts were permeated with fantasies and errors, but still were not to be rejected. One must, he said, show them the respect their age deserved; one must also,

Plate 11. Imagined pasts in the late Renaissance. S. Petri and his fellow
Frisians were far from the only ones to wish to insert themselves into
ancient history. This splendid monument—supposedly the tomb of the
Druid Chyndonax—aroused great interest in the late sixteenth century,
was included in the great corpus of inscriptions illustrated in plate 1
above, and was published with a long and learned commentary in
I. Guénebauld, *Le réveil de Chyndonax* (Dijon, 1621), from which
it is here reproduced.

he insisted, realize that they were not simple fantasies but reworkings, like those of Greek mythology, of real events. A sufficiently critical approach might even enable one someday to disentangle them from their deceptive garb of fantasy and work them up into a straight, factual history of the earliest times. This approach seemed far too tolerant to Casaubon: "I don't see," he wrote in his copy of Scaliger's book, "of what great use these inventions of foolish peoples are to real history."[40]

Scaliger's tolerant attitude, like his critical method, grew like a pearl around one irritating grain of forged matter. This came, however, not from a cosmopolitan classic like Nanni's *Antiquitates* but from the far more provincial work of the antiquaries of nearby Friesland. There earlier sixteenth-century intellectuals had developed a model *Urgeschichte* of the province. They argued that three Indian gentlemen, Friso, Saxo, and Bruno, had left their native country in the fourth century B.C. They studied with Plato, fought for Philip and Alexander of Macedon, and then settled in Frisia, where they drove off the aboriginal giants and founded Groningen.[41] The image is enchanting: three gentlemen in frock coats sitting around a peat fire, murmuring politely in Sanskrit. But around 1600 it inflamed the temper of Ubbo Emmius, a critical humanist Scaliger esteemed. Emmius set out to demolish the story and its supposed basis in written sources. He denounced Friso and his friends as fables. He demanded exact locations for the sources that attested to their existence: "What archives are those? What authors composed the sources? In what language? Where and with whom have they been preserved up to now? Who has seen them?"[42] So much, he scornfully indicated, for the work of Friso's son Scholto, *On the Colonies of the Frisians in Scotland*, and similar nonsense.

Another Frisian intellectual, Suffridus Petri, had given the tale of Friso currency in elegant Latin. He provided it with such traditional forger's safeguards as a supposed archival provenance and lost originals "written in . . . the Frisian language, but in Greek script." Stung and challenged by Emmius, Petri departed from the forger's traditional moves and mounted a brilliant, original defense. He claimed that ancient texts now lost and popular songs like the *carmina* of the early Romans and Germans, long familiar from Livy and Tacitus, could have preserved the origins of Frisia even if formal historians did not. And he insisted that even if such popular sources contained fables, they should be analyzed, not scarified: "A good historian should not simply abandon the antiquities because of the fables, but should cleanse the fables for the sake of the antiquities."[43] Oral tradition, in short, needed critical reworking, not contempt. And only a proper attitude of reverence combined with criticism could result in that.

Scaliger knew these debates because friends of his from Leiden like Janus Dousa plunged into them, trying to cleanse Holland of its origin myths.[44] What is remarkable, again, is his reaction. Like his friend Jacques-Auguste de Thou of Paris, the greatest scholarly historian of the late sixteenth century, he esteemed Emmius highly as a critical scholar after his own model. But nonetheless he imitated Petri. The tolerant and eclectic attitude Petri recommended for Friso informed Scaliger's approach to Berosus and Manetho. When Scaliger published the Babylonian *Urgeschichte* and defended it, as a mythical transfiguration of real events, he used a forger's and a fantasist's tools to integrate the real ancient Near East into the Western tradition. Even if the forger was Petri rather than Nanni, Petri too was a forger who gave philology new intellectual worlds to conquer. Criticism reached so high a level in early modern times, in short, because the challenge and the stimulation of forgery were so acute.

Forgery and philology fell and rose together, in the Renaissance as in Hellenistic Alexandria. Sometimes the forgers were the first to create or restate elegant critical methods; sometimes the philologists beat them to it. And in all cases criticism has been dependent for its development on the stimulus that forgers have provided. Criticism does not exist simply because the condition of the sources creates a need for it. The existence of so many sources created with a conscious intention to deceive, and the cleverness of so many of the deceptions, played a vital role in bringing criticism into being. "It takes a thief to catch a thief" has long been a policeman's proverb; "it takes a forger to expose a fake" might well go alongside it on the wall of the literary detective's study.

EPILOGUE

ONE DAY two women appeared to Hercules. One of them offered him a life of cold baths, great deeds, and suffering, the other a life of luxury, idleness, and pleasure. The first woman identified herself as Virtue and the second as Vice. Though Vice was superficially attractive, Virtue argued with irresistible eloquence that Hercules should follow the harder road that would lead to a higher end. Unfortunately, forgery and criticism resemble one another more closely than vice and virtue, and the choice between them has often proved far more complex and difficult than the one that faced Hercules.

Forgery and criticism both offer ways of dealing with a single general problem. In any complex civilization, a body of authoritative texts takes shape; this offers rules for living and charters for vital social, religious, and political practices. Ways of life and institutions change, but the texts, like Dorian Gray, are eternally youthful. Eventually they clearly fail to correspond with the changed face of the civilization that relies on their guidance.

At this point the intellectuals charged with the interpretation of texts must make choices. They can choose allegory, and explain that while the texts *apparently* do not match the present, that is only because their literal sense masks their true meaning. Only authoritative exegesis can reveal this—and by doing so both preserve the utility of the texts and enhance the authority of the com-

mentators. Or they can choose literalism, and insist that
the modern condition results not from growth but from
corruption. The texts must serve as the basis for a sweep-
ing reform; the face of society will have to be lifted to
match that on the portrait of its youth.

The interpreters can also choose criticism, and explain
that conditions have changed with time, as they always
do. The texts reflected their world, but we live in ours,
which may need a revised set of texts and charters and
can never simply be reformed by the standard of an older
one. Or they can, and often do, mix all of these useful but
incompatible interpretative tactics into a single witches'
brew—a practice usually known in America as constitutional interpretation. Finally, they may forge, and restore
the portrait instead of the face. Evidently forgery is only
one possible way of dealing with the past; it is no more
arbitrary than some of the others. And the structural resemblance between its methods and those of criticism is
reasonable enough, given the more basic resemblance between their immediate practical goals.

Forgery and criticism also share a fundamental limita-
tion. The critic cannot escape time and place any more
than the forger can. The forger imposes personal values
and period assumptions and idioms on his evocation of
the past; that is why his work must eventually cease to
seem credible as what it once purported to be, and becomes instead a document of its own time. But the critic
rejects fakes for personal reasons and on the basis of period assumptions about the world they claim to come
from; that is why at least some of his rejections of texts
will be rejected in their turn. Many ancient and some
later documents have fallen to criticism only to rise again

when the critic's notion of what can and cannot be "classical" or "medieval" reveals its limitations. After all, general assumptions about the past never crystallize. Hence the criticism they govern is doomed to be less a Literary Supreme Court than a Wheel of Textual Fortune—a device for adjusting the past which is necessarily arbitrary and the motion of which is necessarily perpetual. The same description could obviously be applied to forgery itself.

Yet forgery and criticism are hardly identical. The forger seeks to protect himself and us from the critical power of our own past and that of other cultures. He offers us a refuge from the open-ended reflection on our ideals and institutions that a reading of powerful texts may stimulate. Above all, he is irresponsible; however good his ends and elegant his techniques, he lies. It seems inevitable, then, that a culture that tolerates forgery will debase its own intellectual currency, sometimes past redemption—as happened to Hellenistic Greek admirers of forged alien mysteries and modern German admirers of the literature of the Anti-Semitic International.

Criticism is, as we have repeatedly seen, inevitably fallible in its conclusions and deeply indebted to forgery for its methods. It is often undertaken for partial and unscholarly motives. But it seeks not to protect but to expose: to reveal past and foreign cultures as they really were, insofar as we can ever grasp what is not our own. Like the psychoanalyst, the critic sets out to fight the monsters that crowd about us in the long sleep of reason that is human history. Like the psychoanalyst, the critic wields fragile weapons and is constantly betrayed by his own subjectivity. But like the psychoanalyst, the critic practices a profession as vital as it is impossible.[1] The exercise of criticism is a sign of health and virtue in a civilization; the prevalence of forgery is a sign of illness and vice.

A Chinese critic once lamented the impossibility of ever telling forged works from genuine ones centuries after the deaths of their creators: "The ancients are gone, and we cannot raise them from the Netherworld to question them. So how can we arrive at the truth without being vain and false, in our wrangling noisily about it?"[2] The brief examination we have carried out of Western traditions in forgery and scholarship may also seem to warrant despair. But I hope not. I have tried only to do the duty of the critic, to lay bare (rather than ignore or explain away) a fascinating but troubling feature of the Western tradition. The tradition of criticism is to recognize displeasing as well as pleasing features in the sources. We cannot carry on that tradition if we refuse to recognize how much it owes to—and how often it has been implicated in—the activities of its criminal sibling.

NOTES

INTRODUCTION

1. Diogenes Laertius *Lives of the Philosophers* 5.92–93, trans. R. D. Hicks.
2. P. Coleman-Norton, "An Amusing *Agraphon*," *Catholic Biblical Quarterly* 12 (1950): 439–49.
3. See B. M. Metzger, "Literary Forgeries and Canonical Pseudepigrapha," in *New Testament Studies: Philological, Versional, and Patristic* (Leiden, 1980), 1.
4. This area is a very contentious one; for a variety of positions, see N. Brox, *Falsche Verfasserangaben* (Stuttgart, 1975); J. J. Collins, *The Apocalyptic Vision of the Book of Daniel* (n.p., 1977), chap. 3; D. G. Meade, *Pseudonymity and Canon* (Grand Rapids, Mich., 1988). For a similar problem which arises in a very different intellectual tradition, see M. Pereira, *The Alchemical Works Attributed to Raymond Lull* (London, 1989).
5. P. N. Furbank and W. R. Owens, *The Canonisation of Daniel Defoe* (New Haven and London, 1988). The positive ascriptions argued for in this book are, like those it criticizes, not always compelling, but its review of earlier scholarship is fascinating.
6. Those curious may learn about the former case from the amusing popular account by R. Harris, *Selling Hitler* (New York, 1986), and about the latter case from A. Thierry, *Les grandes mystifications littéraires* (Paris, 1911), 243–79.

CHAPTER I

1. J. B. Pritchard, ed., *Ancient Near Eastern Texts Relating to the Old Testament*, 3d ed. (Princeton, 1969), 414, 495.

2. See in general J. Leipoldt and S. Morenz, *Heilige Schriften* (Leipzig, 1953), chap. 3; W. Speyer, *Bücherfunde in der Glaubenswerbung der Antike* (Göttingen, 1970); and cf. the introductory statements in *The Book of Mormon* (Salt Lake City, 1961).

3. *Suda*, s.v. Acousilaos; J. Forsdyke, *Greece before Homer* (London, 1956), 142.

4. Diodorus Siculus 2.32.4.

5. See in general Forsdyke, *Greece before Homer*, chaps. 2–3.

6. F. Jacoby, ed. *Die Fragmente der griechischen Historiker* (hereafter *FrGrHist*), 115 F 154.

7. Cf. A. Momigliano, "Historiography on Written Tradition and Historiography on Oral Tradition," in *Studies in Historiography* (London, 1966), 211–20.

8. Forsdyke, *Greece before Homer*, 44–46. For a much earlier case see Herodotus 5.59–61. The most curious of all these inscribed relics was the collar of a very old deer sacred to Artemis, which recorded that when she was a fawn, Agapenor was at Ilium. This showed, Pausanias remarked, that deer lived even longer than elephants (*Description of Greece* 8.10.10).

9. N. Brox, *Falsche Verfasserangaben* (Stuttgart, 1975).

10. Athenaeus *Deipnosophistae* 1.22d, trans. N. G. Wilson.

11. Galen 17.1.607 Kühn.

12. This causal explanation was offered by Galen 15.105 Kühn. Modern scholars disagree on the basis from which he inferred this—undoubtedly plausible—theory. See, e.g., W. Speyer, *Die literarische Fälschung im heidnischen und christlichen Altertum* (Munich, 1971), 112; W. D. Smith, *The Hippocratic Tradition* (Ithaca and London, 1979), 201; and C. W. Müller, *Die Kurzdialoge der Appendix Platonica* (Munich, 1975), 12–6.

13. See in general R. Pfeiffer, *History of Classical Scholarship from the Beginnings to the End of the Hellenistic Age* (Oxford, 1968); Smith, *Hippocratic Tradition*; K. J. Dover, *Lysias and the Corpus Lysiacum* (Berkeley, 1968); and M. Un-

tersteiner, *Problemi di filologia filosofica* (Milan, 1980), 109–58.

14. See the brilliant account in Speyer, *Fälschung*, 15–17.

15. Dover, *Lysias.*

16. The ancient arguments about the *Rhesus* are discussed in great detail in W. Ritchie, *The Authenticity of the Rhesus of Euripides* (Cambridge, 1964), 1–59; they have fascinated modern scholars since the end of the sixteenth century, when Joseph Scaliger analyzed them in the prolegomena to his edition of Manilius' *Astronomicon*, 3d ed. (Strassburg, 1655), sig. alpha 3 recto. Ritchie traces the debate from the eighteenth century onward. For a more extended ancient essay in higher criticism, which also weighs both internal and external criteria, see Dionysius of Halicarnassus *Lysias* 12.

17. Aulus Gellius *Noctes Atticae* 3.3; see J.E.G. Zetzel, *Latin Textual Criticism in Antiquity* (New York, 1981), 17.

18. See Brox, *Falsche Verfasserangaben*, esp. 105–10.

19. *Letter of Aristeas* 30.

20. See in general J. R. Bartlett, *Jews in the Hellenistic World: Josephus, Aristeas, the Sibylline Oracles, Eupolemus* (Cambridge, 1985), 11–34, for discussion, partial translation, and commentary; there is an edition of the full Greek text of *The Letter of Aristeas* with an English translation by M. Hadas (New York, 1951).

21. Pfeiffer, *History*, 100–101.

22. E. J. Bickerman, *Studies in Jewish and Christian History* (Leiden, 1976), 1: 228–29.

23. *Letter of Aristeas* 29–32.

24. It remains problematic to what extent the supposed authorship of such works mattered to the readers who accepted them; for contrasting views see Brox, *Falsche Verfasserangaben*, and D. G. Meade, *Pseudonymity and Canon* (Grand Rapids, Mich., 1988). See in general G. Bardy, "Faux et fraudes littéraires dans l'antiquité chrétienne," *Revue d'Histoire Ecclésiastique* 32 (1936): 5–23, 275–302.

25. See A. Momigliano, *Alien Wisdom* (Cambridge, 1976).

26. *Corpus Hermeticum* 16.1–2.

27. See chapter 3 below. A still stranger case is that of the Etruscan thunder calendars (explanations of the ominous meaning of thunder on any given day of the year) with which the haruspices predicted the future during the first century B.C. These claimed to be translated word for word from the Etruscan revelations of the primeval demigods Tages and Tarchon— yet another case of texts supposedly written in a sacred language and an unknown script. See E. Rawson, *Intellectual Life in the Late Roman Republic* (London, 1985), 305–6.

28. See the elegant study by E. Champlin, "Serenus Sammonicus," *Harvard Studies in Classical Philology* 85 (1981): 189–212.

29. *Historia Augusta, Tacitus* 8.1–2; *Divus Aurelianus* 1.7.

30. *Historia Augusta, Divus Aurelianus* 2.1, trans. D. Magie. Books and articles on this work have multiplied like rabbits in recent years. For an introduction to the major issues and works, see T. D. Barnes, *The Sources of the Historia Augusta* (Brussels, 1978). And anyone interested in literary forgery will profit from the articles by Sir Ronald Syme collected as *Emperors and Biography: Studies in the Historia Augusta* (Oxford, 1971).

31. Galen *De libris propriis, Opera minora* (Leipzig, 1891), 2:91–124.

32. G. Strohmaier, "Uebersehenes zur Biographie Lukians," *Philologus* 120 (1976): 117–22.

33. Galen 15.12–13 Kühn.

34. Galen 15.172–73 Kühn.

35. To be sure, W. D. Smith argues cogently that Galen's motives had to do not with philological matters but with his basic assumptions about Hippocratic medicine; *Hippocratic Tradition*, 166–72.

36. Eusebius *Historia ecclesiastica* 7.25.

37. See the new edition with French translation and elaborate commentary by N. De Lange, in his edition of Origen, *Lettre à Africanus sur l'histoire de Suzanne* (Paris, 1983), 514–21.

38. Jerome *De viris illustribus* 15; translated and discussed by P. W. Shehan, "St. Jerome and the Canon of the Holy Scriptures," in *A Monument to Saint Jerome*, ed. F. X. Murphy (New York, 1952), 267.

39. Photius *Bibliotheca* cod. 1; for more information on this and later discussions, see I. Hausherr, "Doutes au sujet du 'Divin Denys,'" *Orientalia Christiana Periodica* 2 (1936): 464–50.

40. J. E. Chisholm, *The Pseudo-Augustinian Hypomnesticon against the Pelagians and Celestians* (Fribourg, 1967), 1:41–48. Another nice case of sensitivity to the problems of authenticity and forgery is to be found in the letter by the Carthusian Guigo that listed the pseudepigrapha that had crept into the corpus of Jerome's letters. For the text, see *Patrologia Latina* 153, cols. 593–94; for discussion, see E. F. Rice, Jr., *Saint Jerome in the Renaissance* (Baltimore and London, 1985), 47.

41. Speyer, *Fälschung*, 197–218.

42. J. Trithemius, "Chronologia Mystica," in *Opera historica*, ed. M. Freher (Frankfurt, 1601), vol. 1, sig. ** 5 verso. For a brilliant account of Trithemius' forgeries—and his view of them—see N. Staubach, "Auf der Suche nach der verlorenen Zeit: Die historiographischen Fiktionen des Johannes Trithemius im Lichte seines wissenschaftlichen Selbstverständnisses," in *Fälschungen im Mittelalter*, ed. H. Fuhrmann (Hanover, 1988), 1:263–316.

43. See in general P. Lehmann, *Pseudo-Antike Literatur des Mittelalters* (Leipzig, 1927; repr. Darmstadt, 1964); E. P. Goldschmidt, *Medieval Texts and Their First Appearance in Print* (London, 1943); G. Constable, "Forged Letters in the Middle Ages," in *Fälschungen im Mittelalter*, ed. Fuhrmann, 5:11–38.

44. G. Constable, "Forgery and Plagiarism in the Middle Ages," *Archiv für Diplomatik, Schriftgeschichte, Siegel- und Wappenkunde* 29 (1983): 1–41.

45. M. Clanchy, *From Memory to Written Record: England, 1066–1307* (London, 1979), 254–55; E.A.R. Brown, "*Falsitas pia sive reprehensibilis*: Medieval Forgers and Their Intentions," in *Fälschungen im Mittelalter*, ed. Fuhrman, 1:101–20.

46. B. Guenée, *Histoire et culture historique dans l'Occident mé-
diéval* (Paris, 1980), 133–40. A tendency of recent medieval
scholarship seems to be to emphasize, as Guenée does, the
critical abilities of medieval scholars, and to suggest that
many texts long stigmatized as pure "forgeries" only attained
that status long after their original composition, when they
were used for purposes far from those of their original authors. See in general H. Fuhrmann's untitled lecture in *Fälschungen im Mittelalter*, ed. Fuhrmann, 1:51–58. For a case
study of the *Donation of Constantine* along these lines, see N.
Huyghebaert, "La Donation de Constantin ramenée à ses
véritables dimensions," *Revue d'Histoire Ecclésiastique* 71
(1976): 45–69; and N. Huyghebaert, "Une légende de fonda-
tion: Le *Constitutum Constantini*," *Le Moyen Age* 85
(1979): 177–209, ingeniously arguing that the *Donatio* was
written as a pious narrative designed to instruct pilgrims to
the Lateran in the eighth century. It became a pseudolegal
document only when it was inserted into the false *Decretals*.

47. See in general A. Grafton, "Renaissance Readers and Ancient
Texts: Comments on Some Commentaries," *Renaissance
Quarterly* 38 (1985): 615–49.

48. See in general C. Mitchell, "Archaeology and Romance in
Renaissance Italy,"in *Italian Renaissance Studies*, ed. E. F.
Jacob (London, 1960); C. Mitchell and E. Mandowsky, *Pirro
Ligorio's Roman Antiquities* (London, 1963).

49. For these numbers and some splendid examples—e.g., the
safe-conduct granted to Cicero by Caesar—see F. F. Abbott,
"Some Spurious Inscriptions and Their Authors," *Classical
Philology* 3 (1908): 22–30. For particularly detailed studies
of some especially rich Renaissance forgeries, see J. B. Trapp,
"Ovid's Tomb." *Journal of the Warburg and Courtauld Institutes* 36 (1973): 35–76; P. Pray Bober, "The *Coryciana* and
the Nymph Corycia," *Journal of the Warburg and Courtauld
Institutes* 40 (1977): 223–39; and A. Lintott, "*Acta Antiquis-
sima*: A Week in the History of the Roman Republic," *Papers
of the British School at Rome* 54 (1986): 213–28.

50. L. Delisle, "Cujas déchiffreur de papyrus," in *Mélanges offerts à M. Émile Chatelain* (Paris, 1910), 486–91.
51. For Nanni, see chapters 2 and 4 below. The ingenious Alfonso Ceccarelli tried his skillful hand at virtually every kind of forgery; in the course of his checkered career in Rome and Lunigiana he dreamed up fake genealogies for his friends, composed an entire notarial cartulary that set his friends and patrons back in the medieval period of Luni's history, and wrote at least one fake classical text, Caesar's lost *Anti-Catones*. See G. Pistarino, *Una fonte medievale falsa e il suo presunto autore* (Genoa, 1958).
52. For a text of Valla's work and a study of its context, see W. Setz, *Lorenzo Vallas Schrift gegen die Konstantinische Schenkung* (Tübingen, 1975); for an analysis, see V. de Caprio, "Retorica e ideologia nella Declamatio di Lorenzo Valla sulla donazione di Costantino," *Paragone* 29 (1978): 36–51; for the afterlife of the work, see G. Antonazzi, *Lorenzo Valla e la polemica sulla Donazione di Costantino* (Rome, 1985).
53. Mitchell, "Archaeology and Romance." Agustín's work was entitled *Dialogos de medallas, inscriciones y otras antiguedades* (Tarragona, 1587).
54. C. W. Müller, "Die neuplatonischen Aristoteleskommentatoren über die Ursachen der Pseudepigraphie," *Rheinisches Museum für Philologie*, n.s. 112 (1969): 120–26 = *Pseudepigraphie in der heidnischen und jüdisch-christlichen Antike*, ed. N. Brox (Darmstadt, 1977), 264–71; J. Kraye, "The Pseudo-Aristotelian *Theology* in Sixteenth- and Seventeenth-Century Europe," in *Pseudo-Aristotle in the Middle Ages: The Theology and Other Texts*, ed. J. Kraye et al. (London, 1986), 265–86; J. Kraye, "Daniel Heinsius and the Author of *De mundo*," in *The Uses of Greek and Latin: Historical Essays*, ed. A. C. Dionisotti et al. (London, 1988), 171–97.
55. G. Cardano, *Ars curandi parva*, *Opera* (Lyons, 1663), 7:192–93. For *Humors*, see Smith, *Hippocratic Tradition*, 172–75; Speyer, *Fälschung*, 120 n. 7, 321; the main passage is Galen 16.5 Kühn.

56. In addition to the studies already cited, see L. Panizza, "Biography in Italy from the Middle Ages to the Renaissance: Seneca, Pagan or Christian?," *Nouvelles de la République des Lettres* (1984): 47–98; P. G. Schmidt, "Kritische Philologie und pseudoantike Literatur," in *Die Antike-Rezeption in den Wissenschaften während der Renaissance*, ed. A. Buck and K. Heitmann (Weinheim, 1983), 117–28.

57. See A. Grafton, "From *De die natali* to *De emendatione temporum*: The Origins and Setting of Scaliger's Chronology," *Journal of the Warburg and Courtauld Institutes* 48 (1985): 100–143.

58. See respectively J. Bernays, *Joseph Justus Scaliger* (Berlin, 1855), 205–6; P. W. van der Horst, ed., *The Sentences of Pseudo-Phocylides* (Leiden, 1978), 4–6; and H. J. de Jonge, "J. J. Scaliger's *De LXXXV canonibus apostolorum diatribe*," *Lias* 2 (1975): 115–24, 263.

59. See E. Scheibel, ed., *Iosephi Scaligeri Olumpiadon Anagraphe* (Berlin, 1852).

60. G. Pasquali, *Storia della tradizione e critica del testo*, 2d ed. (repr. Florence, 1971), 94–95.

61. M. Pellegrino, "Intorno a 24 omelie falsamente attribuite a s. Massimo di Torino," in *Studia Patristica*, ed. K. Aland and F. L. Cross, Texte und Untersuchungen 63 (Berlin, 1957), 1:134–41.

62. See A. von Harnack, "Die Pfaff'schen Irenäus-Fragmente als Fälschungen Pfaffs nachgewiesen," *Texte und Untersuchungen*, n.s. 5, 3 (1900): 1–69. As Harnack shows, Pfaff's forged fragments called forth a brilliant rebuttal from one of the greatest critics of his time, Scipione Maffei, which settled the matter of their authenticity permanently—though Pfaff himself never admitted that he had forged them.

63. See in general J. Mair, *The Fourth Forger* (London, 1938); I. Haywood, *The Making of History* (Rutherford, Madison, and Teaneck, 1986); and F. J. Stafford, *The Sublime Savage* (Edinburgh, 1988), the latter two with excellent bibliographies.

64. E. Field, reviewing Buell's *Paul Jones, Founder of the American Navy* (New York, 1900) in the official organ of the nascent historical profession, described it as showing "most careful and painstaking research. Mr. Buell has drawn largely from original material." *American Historical Review* 6 (1900–1901): 589. For an amusing exposure, see A. B. Hart, "Imagination in History," *American Historical Review* 15 (1910): 231–32; the whole story is told by M. W. Hamilton, "Augustus C. Buell, Fraudulent Historian," *Pennsylvania Magazine of History and Biography* 80 (1956): 478–92.

65. N. Cohn, *Warrant for Genocide*, 3d ed. (Chico, Calif., 1981).

66. See chapter 2 below.

67. For one fascinating but intractable recent case, see S. Wertheim and P. Sorrentino, eds., *The Correspondence of Stephen Crane* (New York, 1988), 1:6–10; 2:661–92. Another, somewhat more exotic, case is brilliantly treated by H. R. Trevor-Roper in *Hermit of Peking* (London, 1976).

68. See J. Carter and G. Pollard, *An Enquiry into the Nature of Certain Nineteenth-Century Pamphlets*, ed. N. Barker and J. Collins (London, 1983), and N. Barker and J. Collins, *A Sequel to an Enquiry* (London, 1983).

CHAPTER 2

1. N. Cohn, *Warrant for Genocide*, 3d ed. (Chico, Calif., 1981).

2. M. Guarducci, "La cosidetta fibula Praenestina," *Memorie dell' Accademia dei Lincei*, ser. 8, no. 24 (1980): 413–574—a classic study. In the years before literary scholarship became an academic discipline, respectable forgery on a less ambitious scale than Helbig's—like the splendid forged bit of Thomas Browne on mummies, stuffed with Brunonian words like "semisomnous," that helped to build a reputation in bibliography for the young James Crossley—seems almost to have been a rational career move. See S. Wilkin, ed., *Sir Thomas Browne's Works* (London, 1835), 4:273–76, and S. Crompton, "The Late Mr. James Crossley," *The Palatine Note-*

Book 3 (1883): 228. Sir Geoffrey Keynes remarked that Crossley's fragment "is a literary forgery which, judged purely on its own merits, could ill be spared." *A Bibliography of Sir Thomas Browne* (Cambridge, 1924), 235–36.

3. Both James Macpherson's personal life and his many lovingly evoked scenes of women suffering and dying suggest how strong the elements of sadism and masochism in his character were. See H. R. Trevor-Roper, "Wrong but Romantic," *Spectator* (16 March 1985): 14–15, and F. J. Stafford, *The Sublime Savage* (Edinburgh, 1988).

4. W. Speyer, *Die literarische Fälschung im heidnischen und christlichen Altertum* (Munich, 1971), 210–12.

5. It was affection for Bologna and the cause of feminism that led the eighteenth-century antiquary Alessandro Machiavelli to invent—or at least to adorn—the tale of Alessandra Giliani, the assistant to the great anatomist Mondino de' Luzzi, who died tragically at the tender age of nineteen in 1326, after showing that she could prepare the blood vessels perfectly for anatomical demonstrations and paint astonishingly lifelike pictures of them. He provided an eloquent Latin epitaph to bear out his story of her virtues and accomplishments. See A. Machiavelli, *Effemeridi sacro-civili perpetue* (Bologna, 1736), and G. Fantuzzi, *Notizie degli scrittori Bolognesi* (Bologna, 1786), 5:95–101. My thanks to N. Siraisi for this instructive tale and reference.

6. See the revisionist account by D. Ganzel, *Fortune and Men's Eyes* (Oxford, 1982), which provoked a sharp debate; a judicious review of this, with references, is J. W. Velz, "The Collier Controversy Redivivus," *Shakespeare Quarterly* 36 (1985): 106–15. Another and infinitely more vicious case is that described so well in Cohn, *Warrant for Genocide.*

7. For a striking case in point, see J. S. Weiner, *The Piltdown Forgery* (Oxford, 1955; repr. New York, 1980).

8. E. Tigerstedt, "Ioannes Annius and *Graecia Mendax*," in *Classical, Mediaeval, and Renaissance Studies in Honor of Berthold Louis Ullman*, ed. C. Henderson, Jr. (Rome, 1964), 2:293–310.

9. G. Fowden, *The Egyptian Hermes* (Cambridge, 1986).
10. H. R. Trevor-Roper, *Hermit of Peking* (London, 1976). Plenty of other engaging rogues adorn our dishonor roll of forgers. Buell enriched his curriculum vitae with a college degree that he had not earned and Civil War service that he had not performed; Hamon and Ceccarelli were professional scholars whose careers ended on the scaffold.
11. See the masterly study by I. Ševčenko, "The Date and Author of the So-Called Fragments of Toparcha Gothicus," *Dumbarton Oaks Papers* 25 (1971): 115–88.
12. P. S. Allen et al., eds., *Opus Epistolarum Des. Erasmi Roterodami* (Oxford, 1906–1958), 8:40.
13. See H. J. de Jonge, "Erasmus and the *Comma Johanneum*," *Ephemerides theologicae lovanienses* 56 (1980): 381–89; J. Bentley, *Humanists and Holy Writ* (Princeton, 1983); E. F. Rice, Jr., *Saint Jerome in the Renaissance* (Baltimore and London, 1985), chap. 5.
14. Erasmus, "Declarationes ad censuras Facultatis theologiae Parisiensis," in *Opera omnia*, ed. J. Leclerc (Leiden, 1703–1706), vol. 9, col. 917.
15. See S. Seidel Menchi, "Un'opera misconosciuta di Erasmo? Il trattato pseudo-ciprianico '*De duplici martyrio*,'" *Rivista storica italiana* 90 (1978): 709–43; the older treatment by F. Lezius, "Der Verfasser des pseudocyprianischen Tractates de duplici martyrio: Ein Beitrag zur Charakteristik des Erasmus," *Neue Jahrbücher für Deutsche Theologie* 4 (1895): 95–110, 184–243, retains considerable value.
16. Cf. Erasmus' provision by back-translation from the Vulgate of the Greek text of the last six verses of the Apocalypse, in its own way a form of invention of evidence that his manuscripts did not provide. See B. M. Metzger, *The Text of the New Testament*, 2d ed. (Oxford, 1968), 99–100.
17. E. T. Sage, *The Pseudo-Ciceronian Consolatio* (Chicago, 1910); W. McCuaig, *Carlo Sigonio* (Princeton, 1989).
18. Rice, *Jerome in the Renaissance*; M. Baxandall, *The Limewood Sculptors of Renaissance Germany* (New Haven and London, 1980), 59–60.

19. See the fine study by D. S. Taylor, *Thomas Chatterton's Art* (Princeton, 1978).

20. T. Chatterton, "The Acconte of W. Canynges Feast," in *Complete Works*, ed. D. S. Taylor et al. (Oxford, 1971), 1:294.

21. See I. Haywood, *The Making of History* (Rutherford, Madison, and Teaneck, 1986).

22. G. Nanni, *Commentaria*, 36. (I use the texts in the first edition, Rome, 1498, but cite the page numbers of the better-organized Antwerp, 1552 edition.) For Nanni's methods as a literary forger, see the fine study by E. Fumagalli, "Un falso tardo-quattrocentesco: Lo pseudo-Catone di Annio da Viterbo," in *Vestigia: Studi in onore di Giuseppe Billanovich*, ed. R. Avesani et al. (Rome, 1984), 1:337–60.

23. R. Weiss, "An Unknown Epigraphic Tract by Annius of Viterbo," in *Italian Studies Presented to E. R. Vincent* (Cambridge, 1962), 101–20.

24. Herodotus 5.59.

25. J. R. Bartlett, *Jews in the Hellenistic World: Josephus, Aristeas, the Sibyline Oracles, Eupolemus* (Cambridge, 1985).

26. Yü Ho (A.D. 470), quoted by W. Fong, "The Problem of Forgeries in Chinese Painting," *Artibus Asiae* 25 (1962): 95–119.

27. J. Mair, *The Fourth Forger* (London, 1938).

28. Chatterton, *Works*, ed. Taylor, 845; cf. 854.

29. L. Stephen, *Hours in a Library* (London, 1917), 1:1–43; G. Kitson Clark, *The Critical Historian* (New York, 1967), 67–69.

30. Nanni, *Commentaria*, 463, 15; Diogenes Laertius 1.1.

31. O. A. Danielsson, "Annius von Viterbo über die Gründungsgeschichte Roms," in *Corolla Archaeologica* (Lund, 1932), 1–16; this study remains immensely valuable.

32. Dionysius of Halicarnassus *Antiquitates Romanae*, trans. L. Birago (Treviso, 1480), 1.63: "Quoniam autem incorruptae extant regulae: quibus usus est Eratosthenes."

33. For a typology, cf. Fong, "Problem of Forgeries," which offers many fascinating parallels with and contrasts to the Western tradition of literary forgery. See also the classic essay

of H. Tietze, "Zur Psychologie and Ästhetik der Kunstfäl-
schung," *Zeitschrift für Ästhetik und Allgemeine Kunstwis-
senschaft* 27 (1933): 209–40.

34. I. Casaubon, marginal note in his copy of the *Hermetic Corpus* (Paris, 1554), British Library 491.d.14, 90.

35. J. Perizonius, "Dissertatio de Historia Belli Troiani quae
Dictyos Cretensis nomen praefert," cap. 27, in *Dictys Cretensis et Dares Phrygius de bello Troiano* (London, 1825), 45.
For a different method that arrives at a similar end, see the
interesting 1583 letter of Robert Batt on the Ciceronian *Consolatio*, which argues that it quotes too much real Cicero to be
real itself; published in *Gabriel Harvey's Marginalia*, ed.
G. C. Moore Smith (Stratford-upon-Avon, 1913), 45.

36. J. B. Mencke's comic review of the foibles of scholars, including their gullibility when confronted with fakes, first appeared in Latin as *De charlataneria eruditorum declama-
tiones duae* (Leipzig, 1715); the motto on the frontispiece
of the French edition (plate 8) regularizes the Latin. There
is also an English translation: J. B. Mencke, *The Charlatanry
of the Learned*, trans. F. E. Litz, ed. H. L. Mencken (New
York, 1937); for the context and meaning of the work, see
A. Grafton, "The World of the Polyhistors: Humanism
and Encyclopedism," *Central European History* 18 (1985):
31–47.

37. G. Bagnani, "On Fakes and Forgeries," *Phoenix* 14 (1960):
228–244.

CHAPTER 3

1. See in general A. Grafton, "Polyhistor into *Philolog*: Notes on
the Transformation of German Classical Scholarship, 1780–
1850," *History of Universities* 3 (1983 [1984]): 159–92.

2. W. Speyer, *Die literarische Fälschung im heidnischen und
christlichen Altertum* (Munich, 1971); cf. the critique of
Speyer by E. J. Bickerman, "Faux littéraires dans l'antiquité
classique: En marge d'un livre récent," *Rivista di filologia e di
istruzione classica* 101 (1973): 23.

3. J. Kraye, "Daniel Heinsius and the Author of *De mundo*," in *The Uses of Greek and Latin: Historical Essays*, ed. A. C. Dionisotti et al. (London, 1988), 171–97.

4. A. D. Momigliano, "Ancient History and the Antiquarian," in *Studies in Historiography* (London, 1966), 1–39; L. Gossman, *Medievalism and the Ideologies of the Enlightenment* (Baltimore, 1968); J. Levine, *Doctor Woodward's Shield* (Berkeley, 1977); M. Sina, *Vico e Le Clerc: Tra filosofia e filologia* (Naples, 1978); M. C. Pitassi, *Entre croire et savoir: Le problème de la méthode critique chez Jean Leclerc* (Leiden, 1987); M. Weitlauff, "Die Mauriner und ihr historisch-kritisches Werk," in *Historische Kritik in der Theologie: Beiträge zu ihrer Geschichte*, ed. G. Schwaiger (Göttingen, 1980), 153–209; C. O. Brink, *English Classical Scholarship* (Cambridge and New York, 1986), 133–38.

5. A. Grafton, "Sleuths and Analysts," *Times Literary Supplement* (8 August 1986): 867–68; R. Bentley, *Epistola ad Joannem Millium*, ed. G. P. Goold (Toronto, 1962), 31, 35.

6. J. J. Scaliger, *Epistolae omnes quae reperiri potuerunt*, ed. D. Heinsius (Leiden, 1627), 303–4. For an instructive case study in early modern scholarship in this area, see H. J. de Jonge, "Die Patriarchentestamente von Roger Bacon bis Richard Simon," in *Studies on the Testaments of the Twelve Patriarchs*, ed. M. de Jonge (Leiden, 1975). See also A. Taylor and F. J. Mosher, *The Bibliographical History of Anonyma and Pseudepigrapha* (Chicago, 1951).

7. Scaliger, *Epistolae*, 117–18, 826. See J. H. Meter, *The Literary Theories of Daniel Heinsius* (Assen, 1984), 19–21.

8. On Porphyry, see in general J. Geffcken, *The Last Days of Greco-Roman Paganism*, trans. S. MacCormack (Amsterdam, 1978), 56–81; R. L. Wilken, *The Christians as the Romans Saw Them* (New Haven and London, 1984), chap. 6.

9. I. Casaubon, *Ephemerides*, ed. J. Russell (Oxford, 1850), 1:4.

10. The standard work on Casaubon remains M. Pattison, *Isaac Casaubon, 1559–1614*, 2d ed. (Oxford, 1892). On his work as a scholar, see J. Glucker, "Casaubon's Aristotle," *Classica et Medievalia* 25 (1964): 274–96; Aeschylus, *Agamemnon*,

ed. E. Fraenkel (Oxford, 1950), 1:36–38, 62–78; M. Mund-Dopchie, *La survie d'Eschyle à la Renaissance* (Louvain, 1984), chap. 14.

11. See in general *Die Religion in Geschichte und Gegenwart*, 3d ed., s.n. Reitzenstein, Richard, by C. Colpe; see also A. F. Verheule, *Wilhelm Bousset* (Amsterdam, 1973).

12. Eusebius *Praeparatio evangelica* 10.3.

13. Augustine *Epistola* 102; I use the translation given by Wilken, *Christians*, 143.

14. Porphyry, *"Gegen die Christen,"* 15 *Bücher: Zeugnisse, Fragmente und Referate*, ed. A. von Harnack, Abhandlungen der Königlich Preussischen Akademie der Wissenschaften, philosophisch-historische Klasse (1916), 67–68, frag. 43, from the prologue to Jerome's commentary on Daniel.

15. Ibid. Porphyry's use of Syrian Christian traditions is discussed by P. M. Casey, "Porphyry and the Origin of the Book of Daniel," *Journal of Theological Studies*, n.s. 27 (1976): 15–33; see also Wilken, *Christians*, chap. 6.

16. See also W. Den Boer, "A Pagan Historian and His Enemies: Porphyry against the Christians," *Classical Philology* 69 (1974): 198–208; B. Croke, "Porphyry's Anti-Christian Chronology," *Journal of Theological Studies*, n.s. 34 (1983): 168–69.

17. Diogenes Laertius, *De vitis, dogm. et apophth. clarorum philosophorum, libri x*, ed. I. Casaubon, 2d ed. (Geneva, 1593), *Notae*, 9.

18. Casaubon, manuscript note in his copy of H. Estienne's *Poetae Graeci* (Geneva, 1566), now Cambridge University Library, shelf-mark Adv.a.3.3, 1:726.

19. I. Casaubon, ed., *Historiae Augustae Scriptores sex* (Paris, 1603), *Emendationes ac notae*, 3–4; *Prolegomena*, sig. e ii verso.

20. I. Casaubon, ed., *Theophrasti Notationes morum* (Lyons, 1617), 83–86; B. *Gregorii Nysseni ad Eustathiam, Ambrosiam et Basilissam epistola* (Paris, 1606), dedication and 91.

21. Estienne's note on the diction of the text is at *Poetae Graeci* 2:488; Casaubon underlined it.

22. See J. P. Mahé, *Hermès en Haute-Égypte* (Quebec, 1978–1982), 2:11–13; J. Duchesne-Guillemin, *The Western Response to Zoroaster* (Oxford, 1958), 70, 73, 96–97; C. Colpe, *Die religionsgeschichtliche Schule* (Göttingen, 1961), 10–53; W. C. Grese, *Corpus Hermeticum XIII and Early Christian Literature* (Leiden, 1979), 34–58; G. Fowden, *The Egyptian Hermes* (Cambridge, 1986), xiv.

23. R. Reitzenstein, *Die Hellenistischen Mysterienreligionen*, 3d ed. (Berlin and Leipzig, 1927), 64; *Hellenistic Mystery-Religions*, trans. J. E. Steely (Pittsburgh, 1978), 62.

24. Porphyry *Vita Plotini* 16; *Plotinus*, ed. and trans. A. Armstrong (Cambridge, Mass., 1966), 1:44–45.

25. See in general G. Cozzi, *Paolo Sarpi tra Venezia e l'Europa* (Turin, 1979), 3–133.

26. Reitzenstein, *Mysterienreligionen*, 423–24; *Mystery-Religions*, 540–42.

27. See in general Fowden, *Egyptian Hermes*.

28. The first edition appeared at Treviso in 1471. For recent, contrasting treatments of Ficino's Hermetism and its context, see E. Garin, *Ermetismo del Rinascimento* (Rome, 1988), and M.J.B. Allen, "Marsile Ficin, Hermès et le Corpus Hermeticum," in *Présence d'Hermès Trismégiste* (Paris, 1988), 110–19.

29. P. Crinito, *De honesta disciplina*, ed. C. Angeleri (Rome, 1955); J. Lipsius, *Epistolarum selectarum centuria prima miscellanea* (Antwerp, 1605), 117 (ep. 99).

30. Iamblichus *De mysteriis* 8.4.

31. I. Casaubon, *De rebus sacris et ecclesiasticis exercitationes xvi* (Geneva, 1663), 79.

32. Ibid.

33. Ibid., 72.

34. Ibid., 79.

35. See A. Grafton, "Protestant versus Prophet: Isaac Casaubon on Hermes Trismegistus," *Journal of the Warburg and Courtauld Institutes* 46 (1983): 87–88. This article describes the episode in more detail, and includes the more significant of

Casaubon's notes in his working copy of the *Corpus* (now British Library 491.d.14).

36. Reitzenstein, *Mysterienreligionen*, Beilage xv; *Mystery-Religions*, Appendix xv.

37. See Grafton, "Protestant versus Prophet," 86. Casaubon's copy of Beroaldus' *Chronicum* (Geneva, 1575) is in the British Library, shelf-mark C.79.e.12 (1).

38. Casaubon, *Exercitationes*, 66.

39. Duchesne-Guillemin, *Western Response to Zoroaster*, 10–11.

40. J. Opsopoeus, ed., *Sibyllina Oracula* (Paris, 1599), preface.

41. Cicero *De divinatione* 2.54.110–12.

42. A. I. Baumgarten, *The Phoenician History of Philo of Byblos* (Leiden, 1981), esp. 41; Baumgarten sees Porphyry himself as the probable inventor of much of this (see, e.g., 55).

43. Eusebius *Praeparatio evangelica* 4.5, as modified from Gifford's translation by Wilken, *Christians*, 150; Porphyry, *De philosophia ex oraculis haurienda librorum reliquiae*, ed. G. Wolff (Berlin, 1856; repr. Hildesheim, 1962), 109. It is hazardous to ascribe Porphyry's method here solely to his youth, as some have. Porphyry's account—preserved only in Arabic—of the transmission of the 280 authentic books of Pythagoras is also fanciful; see A. Pauly, G. Wissowa et al., eds., *Realencyclopädie der klassischen Altertumswissenschaft* (1893ff.), supplementary vol. 10, s.n. Pythagoras, by B. L. van der Waerden, and N. Brox, *Falsche Verfasserangaben* (Stuttgart, 1975), 66–67; he describes a small group of wise men who collected and preserved them, in Italy—just the sort of origin story he could have demolished had he wished to.

44. Bodleian Library MS Casaubon 60, fols. 247 recto–253 recto. For another nice example of the motivation of criticism by a theological rather than a philosophical consideration, cf. the attacks on the Kabbalah by sixteenth- and seventeenth-century Jewish scholars. Some of these men argued elegantly that the purportedly ancient texts must in fact be recent because they revealed the influence of late Neo-platonism. See

M. Idel, "Differing Conceptions of Kabbalah in the Early 17th century," in *Jewish Thought in the Seventeenth Century*, ed. I. Twersky et al. (Cambridge, Mass., and London, 1987), 137–200, and M. Idel, *Kabbalah: New Perspectives* (New Haven and London, 1988), 2–3, for this example of the penetration of humanist methods into a new environment. Yet at least one of the critics, Leon Modena, set out to attack the *Zohar* not simply because he saw it was a forgery but because the Kabbalists had angered him with their attacks on Maimonides: *The Autobiography of a Seventeenth-Century Venetian Rabbi*, trans. and ed. M. R. Cohen (Princeton, 1988), 153.

45. W. King, *Dialogues of the Dead* 7, "Chronology," in *A Miscellany of the Wits*, ed. K. N. Colville (London, 1920), 61–62.

CHAPTER 4

1. *Scaligerana* (Cologne, 1695), 123.
2. For Berosus, see *FrGrHist* 680 F 1; there is a modern translation and commentary by S. M. Burstein (1978). For the general context, see S. K. Eddy, *The King Is Dead* (Lincoln, Neb., 1961).
3. J. J. Scaliger, *Lettres françaises inédites*, ed. P. Tamizey de Larroque (Agen and Paris, 1879), 161.
4. Leiden University Library MS Scaligeranus 10, fol. 2 recto, quoting Helladius from Photius *Bibliotheca* cod. 279, and Tatian *Ad Graecos* 36 (= Eusebius *Praeparatio evangelica* 10.11.8 = *FrGrHist* 680 T 2).
5. *Thesaurus temporum*, 2d ed. (Amsterdam, 1658), *Notae in Graeca Eusebii*, 407–8.
6. Bodleian Library MS Casaubon 32, fol. 52 verso.
7. Scaliger, *Notae in Graeca Eusebii*, 408.
8. See the justly influential works of P. Burke, *The Renaissance Sense of the Past* (New York, 1970); J. Franklin, *Jean Bodin and the Sixteenth-Century Revolution in the Methodology of Law and History* (New York and London, 1963); M. P. Gilmore, *Humanists and Jurists* (Cambridge, Mass., 1963);

D. R. Kelley, *Foundations of Modern Historical Scholarship* (New York and London, 1970).

9. K. O. Müller, *Kleine deutsche Schriften* (Breslau, 1847), 1:445-52.

10. W. Goez, "Die Anfänge der historischen Methoden-Reflexion im italienischen Humanismus," in *Geschichte in der Gegenwart: Festschrift für Kurt Kluxen*, ed. E. Heinen and H. J. Schoeps (Paderborn, 1972), 3-21; W. Goez, "Die Anfänge der historischen Methoden-Reflexion in der italienischen Renaissance und ihre Aufnahme in der Geschichtsschreibung des deutschen Humanismus," *Archiv für Kulturgeschichte* 56 (1974): 25-48.

11. W. Stephens, Jr., "The Etruscans and the Ancient Theology in Annius of Viterbo," in *Umanesimo a Roma nel Quattrocento*, ed. P. Brezzi et al. (New York and Rome, 1984), 309-22; W. Stephens, Jr., "*De historia gigantum*: Theological Anthropology before Rabelais," *Traditio* 40 (1984): 43-89, esp. 70-89; C. Ligota, "Annius of Viterbo and Historical Method," *Journal of the Warburg and Courtauld Institutes* 50 (1987): 44-56.

12. As noted above, I use the texts in the first edition of Nanni's *Commentaria* (Rome, 1498), but cite them by the page numbers of the well-edited and well-indexed Antwerp 1552 edition; in this case, 239.

13. Ibid., 460, 75-76, 281.

14. Ibid., 244.

15. Stephens, "Etruscans and the Ancient Theology."

16. Josephus *Contra Apionem* 1.8-10. See in general J. R. Bartlett, *Jews in the Hellenistic World: Josephus, Aristeas, the Sibylline Oracles, Eupolemus* (Cambridge, 1985), 86-89; I quote the passage in his translation, ibid., 171-76, which is accompanied by helpful notes.

17. Josephus *Contra Apionem* 1.130, 1.107, 1.28.

18. Nanni, *Commentaria*, 240.

19. See esp. the classic essay of F. von Bezold, "Zur Entstehungsgeschichte der historischen Methodik," in *Aus Mittelalter und Renaissance* (Munich and Berlin, 1918), 362-83.

20. See W. J. Bouwsma, *Concordia Mundi* (Cambridge, Mass., 1957); H. J. Erasmus, *The Origins of Rome in Historiography from Petrarch to Perizonius* (Assen, 1962).

21. G. Postel, *Le thrésor des prophéties de l'univers*, ed. F. Secret (The Hague, 1969), 67; cf. 76.

22. F. Baudouin, *De institutione historiae universae et eius cum iurisprudentia coniunctione prolegomenôn libri duo* (Paris, 1561), 48–49.

23. J. Caius, *De antiquitate Cantabrigiensis Academiae libri duo* (London, 1568), 21–25; Caius' etymology for "giant" is ancient. For his very modern approach to other philological questions, see V. Nutton, "John Caius and the Eton Galen: Medical Philology in the Renaissance," *Medizinhistorisches Journal* 20 (1985): 227–52; for the Oxford-Cambridge debate (a distant ancestor of the Boat Race), see T. D. Kendrick, *British Antiquity* (London, 1950).

24. See respectively J. Sleidanus, *De quatuor monarchiis libri tres* (Leiden, 1669), 11; Franklin, *Jean Bodin*, 124–25; H. Savile, "Prooemium Mathematicum," Bodleian Library MS Savile 29, fol. 32 recto, where a reference to Berosus' *defloratio* of Chaldean history is underlined and bracketed. Second thoughts?

25. M. Cano, *Loci theologici* 11.6, in *Opera* (Venice, 1776), 234; G. Barreiros, *Censura in quendam auctorem qui sub falsa inscriptione Berosi Chaldaei circunfertur* (Rome, 1565), 26–30.

26. Barreiros, *Censura*, 35–37; V. Borghini, *Discorsi* (Florence, 1584–1585), 1:229.

27. Barreiros, *Censura*, 56–59 (where Barreiros' own chronology seems shaky).

28. Cano, *Opera*, 230–32.

29. Ptolemy *Almagest* 5.14.

30. J. Funck, *Commentariorum in praecedentem chronologiam libri decem* (Wittenberg, 1601), fol. B iiij recto.

31. Ibid., fol. [B v] verso.

32. Ibid., fol. [A v] verso.

33. J. Bodin, *Methodus ad facilem historiarum cognitionem*, cap. x, in *Oeuvres philosophiques*, ed. P. Mesnard (Paris, 1951), 254–57.
34. Ibid., cap. iv, 126.
35. Ibid., cap. viii, 240. For a modern view of Ctesias, see R. Drews, *The Greek Accounts of Near Eastern History* (Cambridge, Mass., 1973), 103–16 (e.g., 109: "all the details were invented").
36. J. Goropius Becanus, *Origines Antwerpianae* (Antwerp, 1569), 357–62. Goropius identified the real source in question as a fragment of Theopompus' *Philippica*, Book 43, preserved in Clement of Alexandria's *Stromateis* 1.117.8 = *FrGrHist* 115 F 205.
37. Goropius, *Origines*, dedication.
38. N. Swerdlow, "Pseudodoxia Copernicana: or, Enquiries into Very Many Received Tenets and Commonly Presumed Truths, Mostly Concerning Spheres," *Archives internationales pour l'histoire des sciences* 26 (1976): 108–58.
39. See A. Grafton, "Higher Criticism Ancient and Modern: The Lamentable Deaths of Hermes and the Sibyls," in *The Uses of Greek and Latin: Historical Essays*, ed. A. C. Dionisotti et al. (London, 1988), 155–70.
40. I. Casaubon, marginal note in his copy of the *Thesaurus temporum* (Leiden, 1606), now Cambridge University Library Adv. a.3.4, *Isagogici canones*, 309: "Ego non video quae magna utilitas sit ad historiam veram in istis stultarum gentium figmentis" (the comment is a reaction to Scaliger's treatment of Manetho's Egyptian dynasty lists).
41. For a summary of this *Urgeschichte*, see S. Petri, *Apologia . . . pro antiquitate et origine Frisiorum* (Franeker, 1603), 15–17.
42. U. Emmius, "De origine atque antiquitatibus Frisiorum," in *Rerum Frisicarum historia* (Leiden, 1616), 7ff.
43. Petri, *Apologia*, 40–41.
44. See in general S. Schama, *The Embarrassment of Riches* (New York, 1987), chap. 2; on Petri and Emmius, see E. H. Waterbolk, "Zeventiende-eeuwers in de Republiek over de grond-

slagen van het geschiedverhaal: Mondelinge of schriftelijke overlevering," *Bijdragen voor de Geschiedenis der Nederlanden* 12 (1957): 26–44; E. H. Waterbolk, "Reacties op het historisch pyrrhonisme," *Bijdragen voor de Geschiedenis der Nederlanden* 15 (1960): 81–102; and Erasmus, *Origins of Rome.*

EPILOGUE

1. Cf. J. Malcom, *Psychoanalysis: The Impossible Profession* (New York, 1981).
2. Lu Shih-hua, quoted by W. Fong, "The Problem of Forgeries in Chinese Painting," *Artibus Asiae* 25 (1962): 99 n. 20.

A NOTE ON
FURTHER READING

For a condensed but comprehensive survey of the general history of scholarship in the West, see L. D. Reynolds and N. G. Wilson, *Scribes and Scholars*, 2d ed. (Oxford, 1974), which ranges widely and offers helpful guidance to the monographic literature. More detailed accounts are provided by the old but informative *History of Classical Scholarship* by J. E. Sandys (Cambridge, 1903–1908), and the two more recent volumes by R. Pfeiffer, *History of Classical Scholarship from the Beginnings to the End of the Hellenistic Age* (Oxford, 1968) and *History of Classical Scholarship from 1300 to 1850* (Oxford, 1976), best consulted in the revised German edition, *Die Klassische Philologie von Petrarca bis Mommsen* (Munich, 1982).

The best single prospect of the whole history of forgery, as I have said before, is afforded by W. Speyer's *Die literarische Fälschung im heidnischen und christlichen Altertum* (Munich, 1971), which includes much material on modern forgery (and criticism) as well as their earlier counterparts. N. Brox offers a lucid and helpfully skeptical supplementary account in *Falsche Verfasserangaben* (Stuttgart, 1975). The older compilation by J. A. Farrer, *Literary Forger* (London, 1907), is broad-gauged and informative, though generally antiquated on points of detail. The most stimulating general treatments in English are G. Bagnani, "On Fakes and Forgeries," *Phoenix* 14

(1960): 228–244, and R. Syme, "Fiction and Credulity," in his *Emperors and Biography: Studies in the Historia Augusta* (Oxford, 1971). The best recent survey in English is B. M. Metzger, "Literary Forgeries and Canonical Pseudepigrapha," in *New Testament Studies: Philological, Versional, and Patristic* (Leiden, 1980), 1–22; see also D. G. Meade, *Pseudonymity and Canon* (Grand Rapids, Mich., 1988). both have good bibliographies. Some of the more original and influential articles on forgery in the ancient world are collected in *Pseudepigraphie in der heidnischen und jüdisch-christlichen Antike*, ed. N. Brox (Darmstadt, 1977).

On medieval forgery, see in general P. Lehmann, *Pseudo-Antike Literatur des Mittelalters* (Leipzig, 1927; repr. Darmstadt, 1964); H. Fuhrmann, "Die Fälschungen im Mittelalter," *Historische Zeitschrift* 197 (1963): 529–554; G. Constable, "Forgery and Plagiarism in the Middle Ages," *Archiv für Diplomatik, Schriftgeschichte, Siegel - und Wappenkunde* 29 (1983): 1–41; and P. Meyvaert, "Medieval Forgers and Modern Scholars: Tests of Ingenuity," in *The Role of the Book in Medieval Culture*, ed. P. Ganz (Turnhout, 1986), 1:83–95.

For forgery and its neighbors in Renaissance culture, the most insightful general treatment remains C. Mitchell, "Archaeology and Romance in Renaissance Italy," in *Italian Renaissance Studies*, ed. E. F. Jacob (London, 1960); for criticism, see the contrasting general accounts of P. G. Schmidt, "Kritische Philologie und pseudoantike Literatur," in *Die Antike-Rezeption in den Wissenschaften während der Renaissance*, ed. A. Buck and K. Heitmann (Weinheim, 1983), and A. Grafton, "Higher Criticism Ancient and Modern: The Lamentable Deaths of Hermes and the Sibyls," in *The Uses of Greek and Latin: Historical Essays*, ed. A. C. Dionisotti et al. (London, 1988).

On the new pasts invented in the seventeenth and eighteenth centuries, see in general I. Haywood, *The Making of History* (Rutherford, Madison, and Teaneck, 1986). An invaluable guide to the Enlightenment's new forms of historical consciousness is L. Gossman's *Medievalism and the Ideologies of the Enlightenment* (Baltimore, 1968). Perhaps the deepest study of a modern forger is that found in the notes to D. S. Taylor's edition of Chatterton's *Complete Works* (Oxford, 1971); see also his fine work, *Thomas Chatterton's Art* (Princeton, 1978). I. Haywood's *Faking It* (Brighton, 1987) summarizes the argument of his larger book and briefly considers both some more recent literary forgeries and the related question, into which I cannot enter here, of the forgery of works of art. See also the far more elaborate, and still stimulating, treatment of the latter topic by O. Kurz: *Fakes*, 2d ed. (New York, 1967).

No single work surveys all the methods of detection applied by modern critics, but R. D. Altick's *The Scholar Adventurers* (New York, 1950) vividly describes a number of them as applied in specific episodes. Finally, the British Museum forgery show of 1990 will present the largest assembly yet made of forged texts and objects. Its catalogue (by N. Barker) will not only reproduce many of these but also provide further information on many of the literary forgers and critics discussed in this book.

INDEX

INDEX